Withdrawn from circulation

LANDMARK VISITORS GUIDE

Dominican Republic

Don Philpott

Published by
Landmark Publishing Ltd
Waterloo House, 12 Compton, Ashbourne
Derbyshire, England, DE6 1DA

Don Philpott is a journalist, author and broadcaster who has spent the last thirty years exploring the world as a writer. Born in Hull, England, he worked for twenty years with the Press Association, the UK national news agency. He founded and co-edited Footloose, an outdoor activities magazine and he contributes on a variety of subjects to newspapers and magazines in the UK and USA.

He now lives in Florida and is executive editor of a newspaper and magazine publishing house. He has written more than 50 books on travel, wine, food, diet and health issues and the media.

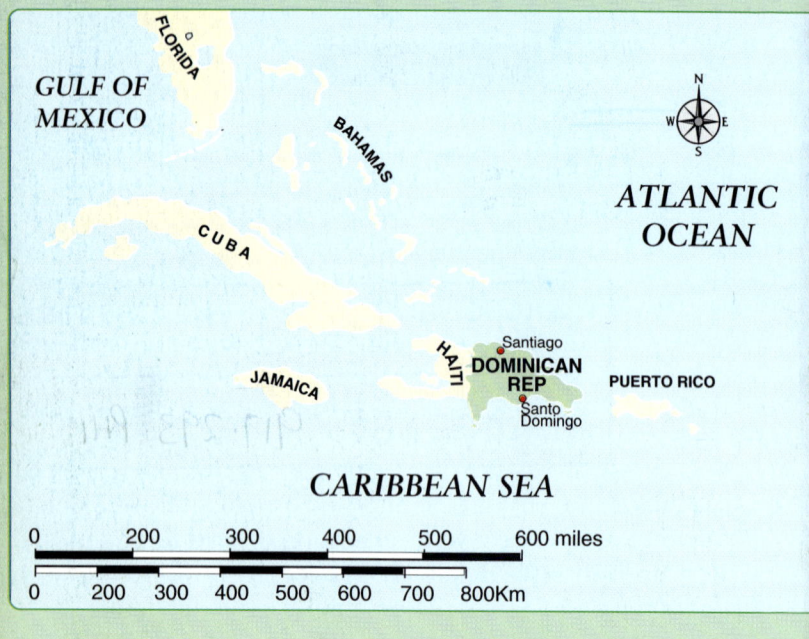

Opposite Page: Casa de Campo beach

Contents

1 WELCOME TO THE DOMINICAN REPUBLIC 6

Introduction 6
Map 10

2 THE HISTORY & LIFE OF THE ISLAND 26

Columbus 26
Indians & Cannibals 28
French occupation 33
Haitian invasion 36
American stewardship 37
Present day 38
People 40
Religion 41
Culture and Festivals 41
Universities 44
Economy 44
The Government and Judiciary 46
Food and drink 46
Rum 63

3 LA CAPITAL: SANTO DOMINGO 66

Location 66
Getting around 67
History 68
The Colonial City - a walking tour 68
Map 70
Exploits of Francis Drake 74
Theatres 82
Eating out in Santo Domingo 84
Nightlife 85

4 EXPLORING & TOURING 86

Getting around 88

Tour 1: The South West and Lake Enriquillo 90

Tour 2: The South East and Punta Cana 96

Tour 3: The Central Highlands and Mount Duarte 104

Tour 4: The Amber Coast 105

4A: The North west and Puetto Plata 108

Tobacco 107
Amber 112

4B: The North East and Semana 115

Whales 117

FactFile

Arrivals	120
Emergency Numbers	120
A to Z of the Dominican Republic	120
Accommodation	120
Airports	121
Airlines	121
Banks	122
Beaches and swimming	123
Buses/ taxis	124
Car Rental/driving	125
Churches	128
Clothing	128
Disabled Facilities	128
Drugs	128
Electricity	129
Embassies and consulates	129
Festivals/Public Holidays	130
Fruits and spices	130

Health	131
Hotels	131
Irritating insects	139
Language	140
Museums	141
National Parks	141
Nightlife	141
Discos and nightclubs	142
Photography	143
Restaurants	144
Security	144
Service Charges	145
Sightseeing and tours	146
Sport	148
Telephones	153
Tourist Offices	154
Tour Operators	155
Weddings	157
Weights and Measures	157

Index 158

WELCOME TO THE DOMINICAN REPUBLIC

Introduction

The Dominican Republican is a tropical paradise that has something for everyone. From the magnificent old city of Santo Domingo to the modern resorts of Puerto Plata and Boca Chica, there is spectacular scenery, a wealth of sporting and other outdoor activities, stunning wildlife and a genuinely warm and friendly people. Discovered by Christopher Columbus in 1492, the explorer wrote in his log: "This is the most beautiful land that human eyes have ever seen."

Occupying more than two-thirds of the historic island of Hispaniola, the Dominican Republic is a country of constant contrasts and changes. Every region has something different with historic sites to be visited, pristine reefs to be explored, wonderful foods to be enjoyed, superb beaches to be lazed on and luxury resorts to be relaxed in.

The landscapes as you drive around the country are breathtaking, even though some of the roads can be a challenge. There are the spectacular central mountains blanketed with tropical forests which are home to scores of exotic birds; Lake Enriquillo to the west has the greatest concentration of American crocodiles in the world and the fertile valleys around Santiago, the country's second largest city, produce the tobacco for some of the world's finest cigars.

A visit to the National Aquarium, Botanic gardens and the National Zoo in Santo Domingo will show just how diverse the island's wildlife is, and how rich the surrounding seas and reefs. So far, more than 300 different types of orchid

Above: *Sun and fun in the Dominican Republic*

alone have been recorded in the country.

Along the north and south coasts, there are some of the most beautiful and secluded beaches to be found in the Caribbean – and some of the finest resorts. The islanders boast that there is only one season – summer, which lasts all year round. The sun almost always shines, the sand is sparkling white and the sea is a stunning turquoise, warm and crystal clear.

The island boasts a wide variety of cuisines, a legacy of its colourful and varied past. While you can enjoy the finest gastronomic food in many of the top restaurants, it is fun to eat out and sample the delicious local fare. Enjoy the freshest of fish cooked in coconut milk, the famed Monte Cristi goats which feed on wild oregano, crabs from Miches and sancocho, a traditional and succulent meat and vegetable stew which varies from town to town.

The Dominican Republic is also a great place for shopping. Santo Domingo has upmarket stores and shopping centres offering local arts and crafts, excellent locally-made shoes and a wide range of leather goods. Paintings and sculptures by local artists make good buys, as do the ceramic, basketry, needle point and cotton goods.

After a day's shopping followed by a good meal, you can dance the night away at one of the many clubs and discos. Dancing, especially the merengue, is a national passion and it is quite common to see couples dancing in the street to the music of a radio perched on a nearby wall. Gradually other passers-by join them, and soon there is a street party as scores of people enjoy the sultry rhythms and the balmy night air. Join in and enjoy all that the Dominican Republic has to offer.

Note: The Dominican Republic should not be confused with the island of Dominica which lies 500 miles (800km) to the south east in the Windward Islands.

Location

The Dominican Republic occupies only the eastern two-thirds of the whole island: the independent republic of **Haiti** occupies the western third. Although it is theoretically possible to visit Haiti from the Dominican side, in reality it is a depressing experience.

The island is situated between Cuba to the west and Puerto Rico to the east. The north and east coastlines face the Atlantic Ocean while the southern coast faces the Caribbean Sea (Mar Caribe). It is larger than the Bahamas, Jamaica, Puerto Rico, all the Virgin Islands and the entire French Indies put together.

Before you go

Make sure that all your travel arrangements are confirmed and that you have a visa if required. Visitors from Britain, North America and the European Community do not need one.

Upon arrival, return air tickets, proof of booked accommodation or adequate financial means are sometimes requested.

For those wishing to buy flight only and make their own arrangements when they arrive, there is a comprehensive list of accommodation of all categories in the FactFile at the back of this book.

When to go

Many people feel that between November and April is the best time to visit the Dominican Republic because it is dryer and cooler. Temperatures, however, do not vary a great deal throughout the year and any time is a great time to visit.

Where to go

There are three main tourist areas: east from Puerto Plata on the north coast, Playa Bavaro on the east coast and along the southern coast between Santo Domingo and Altos de Chavón. Outside these areas and the main cities, there are few tourist facilities, but there is an enormous area of countryside to explore and enjoy.

Getting there

By air

There are two major international airports: Las Américas is located at Punta Caucedo, 20 miles (32km) east of the capital, Santo Domingo; La Unión is at Puerto Plata on the north coast, which is 15 minutes from Playa Dorada, Puerto Plata and Sosúa.

Punta Cana's international airport serves the east and the new Barahona airport serves the south west. The airport at La Romana serves the Casa de Campo resort and the surrounding east. Herrera in Santo Domingo, Arroyo Barril in Samaná, and Santiago can handle small jets, private and charter planes and larger propeller aircraft.

Flying times: New York 3 hours, Miami 2 hours, San Juan 35 mins, Toronto 5 hours, and most European cities 8-10 hours.

ATLANTIC OCEAN

Cabo Frances Viejo

Rio San Juan
Cabrera
MARIA TRINIDAD
ares
UARTE
Bahia Escocesa
Nagua
El Factor
SAMANA
Cabo Cabron
Francisco
Castillo
Cabo Samana
Cama
Yama
Bahia de Samana
HEZ
REZ
Sabana de la Mar
Samana
Grande
HATO MAYOR
Miches
de Boya
El Valle
MONTE PLATA
EL SEIBO
Monte Plata
a Blanca
Hato Mator
Yamasa
El Seibo
LA ALTAGRACIA
DISTRITO
NACIONAL
SAN PEDRO
DEL MACORIS
Guaymate
Higuey
LA
ROMANA
Santo
Domingo
Juan
Dolio
San Pedro
de Macoris
La Romana
Altos de Chavon
Bajos de Haina
San Cristobal
Cabo
Caucedo
San Rafael
del Yuma
Cabo
San Rafael

Punta Palenque

Isla
Catalina

Isla Saona

BBEAN

DOMINICAN
REPUBLIC

11

Main carriers offering schedule services to the Dominican Republic include American Airlines, American Eagle, Aces, Aerotour and Dominican, plus Air France, Air Portugal, Alitalia, Apa International, ALM, Condor, Continental, Copa, Iberia, Ladeco, LTU, Martinair, TWA and Viasa. More than 60 charter companies fly to Puerto Plata, Santo Domingo and Punta Cana from the U.S. Canada, Latin America, Caribbean and Europe.

From the U.S. The national airline, Dominicana, operates flights to San Juan, Puerto Rico, Miami and New York. American Airlines also flies to Santo Domingo, and there are flights from other U.S. cities to Boston, Chicago, Miami and San Juan where connecting flights are available.

From Europe: There are regular scheduled or charter flights from Madrid, Rome, Milan, Lisbon, Paris, Amsterdam, Frankfurt, Bonn, Berlin, Hamburg, Düsseldorf, Munich, Stuttgart, Helsinki, Brussels, London and Glasgow.

Gateways: There are also many flights from European cities to Miami and San Juan where connections can be caught. Caribbean gateways with connections are: Havana, Providenciales (Turks and Caicos), Bonaire, Aruba, Curaçao, Antigua, St. Martin, Kingston and Port-au-Prince. From South America: Bogota, Caracas, Panama City, Santiago de Chile, La Paz, Cancun and Buenos Aires.

From North America: Ottawa, Toronto, Montreal, Quebec City, Halifax, Boston, Dallas, Minneapolis, Detroit, Miami, Newark and New York.

From the Caribbean: Dominicana flies daily to San Juan, Puerto Rico. There are also flights to Curaçao in the Dutch Antilles.

By Sea

Traditionally, all the main ports such as Monte Cristi and Sanchez, were located on the north coast and Samaná Bay – which is still one of the largest and safest natural harbours in the Caribbean.

Today, however, Santo Domingo is the main port, while most sugar is exported through San Pedro de Macoris close to the Haitian border in the north west, and La Romana on the south east coast.

Puerto Plata is the only large commercial port still operating on the north coast, from which agricultural crops such as tobacco, coffee and cacao produced in the Cibao valley are exported. Some bauxite, gypsum and salt is shipped from Barahone on the south west coast.

A new cruise dock is being built in Santo Domingo alongside the Colonial City; Pedro de Macoris may also be added to the itinerary.

Landscape

The Dominican Republic is characterised by miles of stunningly beautiful beaches, towering mountains, rocky cliffs, fertile valleys, cacti-studded desert regions, and more than 992 miles (1600km) of coastline.

Mountains

The countryside is dominated by the towering central highlands, the **Cordillera Central,** with Pico Duarte (Mt Duarte) at 10,417 feet (3176m), being the highest point in the West Indies.

There are five distinct mountain ranges running north west to south east, with the Cordillera Septentrional running parallel with the north west coast, two smaller ranges in the south west, and the Cordillera Oriental (Eastern Highlands) in the north east.

Lakes and rivers

Separating the mountain chains are large fertile valleys, one of which contains **Lake Enriquillo** in the south west.

The island's two main rivers are the **Yaque del Sur**, which runs south from the Central Highlands into the Bahia de Neiba, and the **Yaque del Norte**, which runs north from the highlands into the Bahia de Monti Cristi, and there are some impressive waterfalls.

In the mountains the water is fast-flowing and turbulent; on the plains it meanders gently to the sea. Swimming, however, is not advisable.

The main rivers in the east are the **Rio Yuna** which runs eastwards into the Bahia de Samaná, and the **Rio Ozama** which runs south into the sea on the eastern outskirts of the capital Santo Domingo.

Most of the eastern half of the country consists of plains and gently undulating verdant hills and grasslands, sloping down to the azure sea.

Climate

Temperature

The Dominican Republic lies in the tropics, and although relatively small, has a number of climatic zones largely determined by the mountains.

The annual average temperature is 77F (25C), with summer temperatures rarely rising above 90F (32C) because of the year round influence of the north east trade winds which

13

blow in from the Atlantic. Winter average temperature is 73F (23C) rising to an average summer temperature of 82F (28C). Temperatures cool with altitude, but even in the Central Highlands, the year round average is a humid 69F (21 C).

Rainfall

Rainfall also varies enormously with altitude. Annual rainfall in the north west highlands is highest at more than 100 inches (250cm) a year. As the prevailing winds blow across the island from the north east they deposit most of the rain over the mountains, causing rain shadows west of the north west mountains, and west of the central highlands. In the extreme south west the annual rainfall is only about 30 inches (76cm) which results in arid, near-desert conditions with spectacular stands of cactus.

Hurricanes

The hurricane season lasts from June to November with September and October usually the busiest months for tropical storms. Statistically, only four hurricanes hit the island every 100 years, and the government has detailed contingency plans, including evacuation and storm shelters. If a hurricane threatens, follow the advice given locally.

Above: Bayahibe beach
Opposite Page: A glimpse at the Puerto Plata coast
Below: Samaná Peninsula

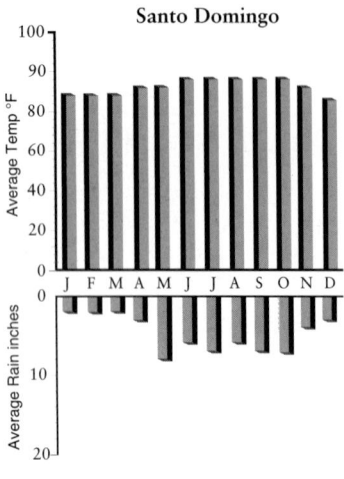

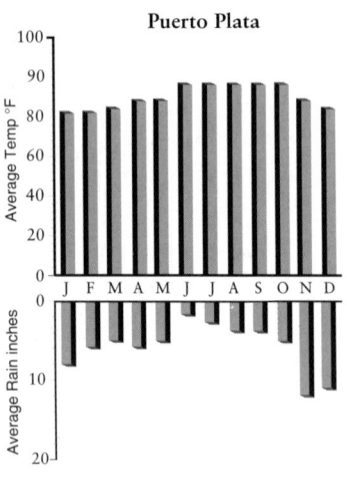

The island is on a geologically active plate, and small submarine earthquakes do occasionally occur.

Plants

Anyone who is interested in nature will love the Dominican Republic.

The island's changing terrain supports an enormous variety of plant and animal life. There are more than 5,600 recorded species of plants, of which more than a third are endemic. The overall impression is of greenery, exotic trees and palms, stunning flowers and dense tropical rain forests. There are coastal mangrove swamps, stretches of cactus-studded desert, and fantastic offshore reefs.

Tropical

Many parts of the island are the very image of a tropical paradise: bougainvillea, hibiscus and frangipani grow in glorious profusion. There are hillsides covered in giant ferns, royal palms, massive stands of towering bamboo, sugar cane, bananas, coconut groves, hanging breadfruit, mango, nutmeg, cacao, pawpaw and the most stunning array of spectacularly coloured flowering plants. Even where the natural vegetation has been cleared for crops, everything is lush and green.

In the countryside, exotic plants grow wild along roadsides and hedgerows: there is the vinelike **caralita**, **calabash** with its gourd-like fruits, **tamarind**, giant **African tulip trees** festooned with scarlet blooms and the distinctive star-shaped leaves of the **castor bean**, whose seeds when crushed yield castor oil.

Flowering plants include the **flamboyant** tree (royal poinciana), with its brilliant red flowers, also known as the tourist tree because it bursts into bloom in early summer, seemingly for the benefit of the visitors. Dark brown seed pods form up to two feet in length after flowering, and can be used as rattles when the seeds have dried out inside.

Growing on the hillslopes are many species of **orchid**, some of them rare and some so tiny that they are easily over looked. More than 300 varieties of orchids have been classified. These include *oncidium henekenii*, which resembles a tiny spider, and *polyradicion lindenii* which looks like a small frog.

The leaves of the **traveller's palm** spread out like a giant open fan. The tree was so named because the fan was believed to point from south to north – but in reality, it rarely does.

Rain Forest

On the mountain slopes are humid tropical rain forests where pines and majestic hardwoods grow in splendour. There is mahogany, satinwood, *lignum vitae* 'the tree of life' and white cedar, swathed with vines and mosses.

Higher altitudes have wind stunted dwarf trees and areas of scrub, fern and coarse grasses.

Gardens

Many Dominicans surround their homes with enviably exotic gardens containing flowers, vegetables and trees. The trees are important both for shade, and because many provide fruit. A wide variety can be seen, including citrus, avocado, sweetsop, soursop, mango, coconut, breadfruit and papaya. Bananas are grown almost everywhere.

Bougainvillea flowers in lush abundance, and seems to be in bloom all year round in a host of different colours. In fact, the colour does not come from petals, but from the plant's bract-like leaves which surround the small petal-less flowers.

There are scores of varieties of hibiscus, frangipani, and poinsettia growing alongside

Above: Sosúa beach
Middle: Aerial shot of Gran Ventana
Below: Don Juan Beach Resort.
Opposite Page: Street scene, Altos de Chavón

exotic vegetables like yam, sweet potato and dasheen. The list of exotic flowers is also endless: heliconia, also known as the lobster plant, bird of paradise flowers, anthurium, yellow and purple allamandas and the multi-coloured ixora.

The flowers attract hummingbirds like the doctorbird, as well as the carib grackle – a strutting, starling-like bird with a paddle-shaped tail, and the friendly bananaquit.

Gardens are also visited by tree lizards and the larger geckos which hunt at night.

Scrubland

Drier areas of scrubland have their own flora and fauna, with plants bursting into colour following the first heavy rains after the dry season.

There are **century** plants, with their prickly, sword like leaves, which grow for up to twenty years before flowering. The yellow flower stalk grows at a tremendous rate for several days and can reach 20 feet (6.1m) high, but having bloomed once the whole plant then dies. Other typical scrubland vegetation includes aloe, acacia, prickly pear and several species of cactus.

Manchineel

The manchineel tree, which can be found on many beaches, has a number of effective defensive mechanisms which can prove very painful.

Trees vary from a few feet to more than 30 feet (9.1m) in height, and have widely spreading, deep forked boughs with small, dark green leaves and yellow stems, and fruit like small green apples.

If the leaves are examined carefully without touching them, small pin-head sized raised dots are noticeable at the junction of the leaf and leaf stalk.

The apple-like fruit is very poisonous, and sap from the tree causes very painfull blisters. It is so toxic, that early Caribs are said to have dipped their arrow heads in it before hunting trips. Sap is released if a leaf or branch is broken, more so after rain. Avoid contact with the tree, don't sit under it, or on a fallen branch, and do not eat the fruit, if you do get sap on your skin, run into the sea and wash it off as quickly as possible.

Desert

In areas of lower rainfall, the vegetation consists of thorn, cactus, yucca, mesquite and squat woodlands. These plants are drought resistant and can survive in a dormant state sometimes for months even after losing all their leaves because of lack of moisture.

Swamp

Along the coast there are swamps, mangroves and marsh woodlands. Over the past 100 years much of the forest that covered the lower slopes of the hills and mountains has been cleared, at first for building materials and fuel, and then by indiscriminate commercial logging.

Beach

Approaching the shoreline, there are red-barked turpentine trees, kapok and bearded figs. Beach morning glory, with its array of pink flowers is found on many beaches, and is important because its roots help prevent sand drift. The plant also produces nectar from glands in the base of its leaf stalks which attract ants, and it is thought this evolution has occurred so that the ants will discourage any leaf-nibbling predators. Other beach plants include seagrape and the manchineel, which should be treated with caution.

Marine life

The sea teems with brilliantly coloured fish and often even more spectacularly coloured coral and marine plants. Even just floating face down in the water with a mask on, you can enjoy many of the beautiful underwater scenes, but the best way to see things is by scuba diving, snorkelling or taking a trip in a glass bottomed boat.

Corals

Scores of different multi-coloured corals make up the reefs offshore. There are hard and soft corals and only one, the **fire coral,** poses a threat to swimmers and divers, because it causes a stinging skin rash if touched. Among the more spectacular corals are deadman's fingers, staghorn, brain coral and seafans. There are huge sea anemones and sponges.

Tropical fish species include the parrotfish, blue tang, surgeonfish, tiny but aggressive damselfish, angelfish and brightly coloured wrasse.

Animals

Wildlife is similarly rich and varied: there are 60 species of amphibian, 141 species of rep-

Above: Cabarete beach **Below:** Riviera Beach Hotel, Barahona

Above: Sosúa beach
Below: Fruit seller on Sosúa beach

tile including the Rhinocerus iguana, Ricord's iguana, and the rare American crocodile; 258 species of birds, 33 species of land mammal and 13 species of marine mammal, including the humpback whale and the manatee.

There are few other large animals because hunting is popular, but there is a rich population of reptiles, insects, butterflies, moths and bats. Alligators and crocodiles can be seen near the mouths of the two Yaque Rivers and at Lake Enriquillo, and many species of lizards and rock climbing iguanas can be seen basking in the sunshine or scuttling into the undergrowth.

The island harbours scorpion and large centipede, hundreds of species of spider, including the "hairy" tarantula, and some huge moths. There are also many types of bat.

Several species of endangered turtle live here – leatherback, hawksbill and green – and offshore, dolphins, whales and manatees can be seen. The humpback whale is a regular visitor. The manatee is the animal which early mariners thought were mermaids – obviously after having been at sea for too long, or having drunk too much local rum!

Coastal swamps also provide a rich habitat for wildlife. Tiny tree crabs and burrowing edible land crabs scurry around in the mud trapped in the roots of mangrove trees just above water level. Herons, egrets, pelicans and often frigatebirds roost in the higher branches, and the mangrove cuckoo shares the lower branches with belted kingfishers.

Birds

The island has a rich birdlife with residents and visiting migrants, but many species, including ducks, are hunted.

Main island species include the bright green Hispaniola parrot, also known as La Cotica, and the Hispaniola woodpecker, Zenaida dove (also known as the mountain dove), the ground dove, hummingbirds such as the Hispaniola emerald hummingbird, and the green throated carib (or doctor bird). There are solitaires and flamingoes, Caribbean elaenia, black witch, kingbird, grackle, thrushie, aggressive pearl-eyed thrasher, mocking bird, bananaquit, grasssquit, smooth-billed ani, Caribbean martin and the hovering killi-killi (American kestrel). The gentle cooing of the zenaida dove is a familiar island noise.

The **ani**, a member of the cuckoo family, is easily

recognised by its dark plumage and parrot-like beak. It is known locally as the black witch and it has a shrill squawking call and strange and impractical nesting habits. The hen birds tend to lay their eggs in a communal nest. The first bird lays her eggs, the second lays her eggs on top and so on. The birds take it in turns to sit on the eggs but the eggs at the bottom of the pile do not get enough body heat for incubation, so rarely hatch.

Offshore you may see tropicbirds and the magnificent **frigatebird**, easily recognisable by its size, with the long black seven to eight foot (2-2.5m) wing span, forked tail and apparent effortless ability to glide on the winds.

There are brown booby birds, named by sailors from the Spanish word for 'fool' because they were so easy to catch.

Pelicans, which look so ungainly on land and yet are so acrobatic in the air, are common, as are laughing gulls and royal terns. Several species of sandpiper can usually be seen scurrying around at the water's edge.

If you are really interested in bird watching, pack a small pair of binoculars. The new mini-binoculars are ideal for island bird watching, because the light is normally so good that you will get a clear image despite the small object lens.

National Parks

The Dominican Republic has five national parks which can be visited with permission. There are two parks in the Central Mountains, and the others are: Isla Cabritos on Lago Enriquillo, Los Haitises on Bahia de Samaná and the Parque Nacional del Este. Permission to visit the parks can be obtained by applying to the National Park Headquarters, Calle las Damas 6, Santo Domingo (☎ 685-1316).

Keen naturalists should visit the Museum of Natural History in Santo Domingo's Cultural Park. It is open from 10.30am to 5.30pm Tuesday to Sunday (☎ 689-0106).

THE HISTORY & LIFE OF THE ISLAND

Columbus

Columbus (Colon in Spanish) was the first European to "discover" the Dominican Republic during his first voyage of exploration in 1492. He approached the island from the north on 5 December, and called the island La Espanola (Little Spain). He thought he had sailed all the way to India so he called the natives who greeted him Indians. The first settlement was the fortress La Navidad, but it was destroyed by Indians who also killed the 40 soldiers garrisoned there.

The first settlement was established at **La Isabela** on the north coast a year later on 2 January, 1494, during Columbus's second voyage of discovery. The first mass in the

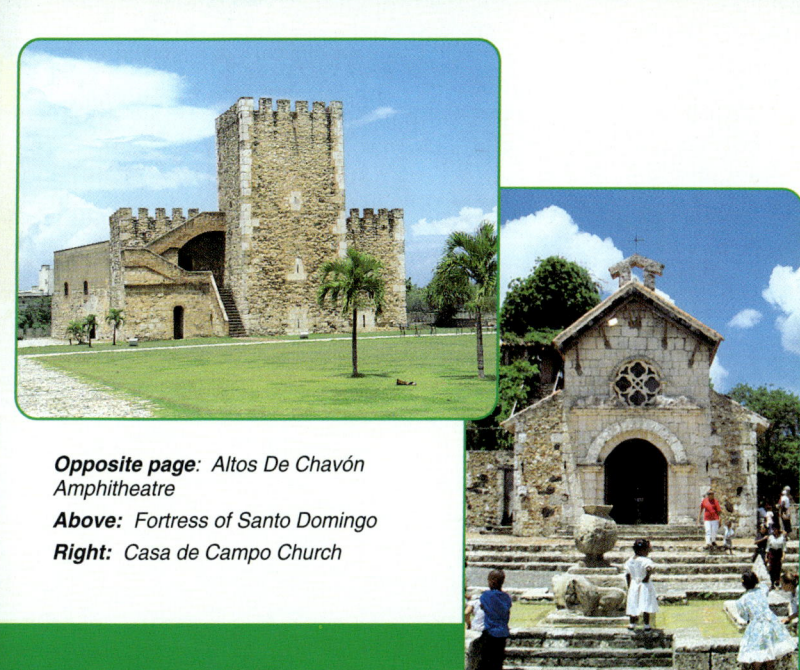

Opposite page: Altos De Chavón Amphitheatre
Above: Fortress of Santo Domingo
Right: Casa de Campo Church

Americas was celebrated there on 6 January. About 1,000 settlers were landed, but the Spanish were repeatedly attacked by the Caribs and their numbers seriously depleted. Many of those not killed by the Indians died from disease and illness because of the unhealthy location.

When Columbus returned, he moved the settlement to the south coast. The site was chosen because it was healthier and more importantly, because it was closer to the gold mines that had been established in the mountains around La Vega. The settlement grew to become the capital **Santo Domingo**. It was to have been called Nueva Isabela but was named Santo Domingo in honour of Columbus's father. It was founded in 1496, making it the oldest European settlement in the Western Hemisphere.

Indians & Cannibals

Long before the Spaniards arrived, the islands had been settled by several different groups of Amerindians ,Taino, Arawak and Caribs (who gave their name to the Caribbean Sea), who had travelled through the Caribbean from South America.

Around AD1000, Arawaks arrived from neighbouring Caribbean islands to the south, to escape the warlike Carib Indians. They called the island **Quisqueya**, which means "Mother of all lands".

The **Arawaks** were a peaceful people who fished and foraged and grew basic crops, such as maize, manioc and peppers. Turtles and iguanas also provided a plentiful source of food. They lived in round thatched 'hurricane proof' huts in small villages ruled by a cacique (chieftain), and were skilled potters, weavers and boatbuilders.

Their dug out canoes were incredibly seaworthy, and their weaving skills were such that they could weave baskets from strips of palms that were totally watertight. The Indians also slept in beds slung between two poles, and the hammock is one of their legacies.

Several **Taino** words still exist such as barbacoa (barbecue), bohio (hut), canoa (canoe) caribe (Caribbean), casabe (cassava), hamaca (hammock), huracán (hurricane), iguana (iguana), lambi (conch meat), maiz (maize), tabaco (tobacco) and yiuca (manioc). They worshipped gods of nature, represented by statues or idols made of wood, stone or bone.

The **Caribs** followed, who were feared warriors. Their battle canoes, powered by a hundred or more paddles, could outrun a sailing ship over a short distance.

The original name of the Caribs was Kalina meaning 'we alone are people'. The Spanish confused this with their word 'cariba', which was short for 'caribales' meaning cannibal, and this was then shortened to Carib.

The Caribs were feared by early European explorers because of horrific stories about cannibalism, with victims being roasted alive on spits. The Caribs were even reported to have a taste preference, thinking Frenchmen were the most tasty, and then the English and Dutch, with the Spanish considered stringy and almost inedible.

Villages were built inland in forest clearings and huts had timber walls and thatched roofs. Early paintings show that they enjoyed dancing, either for pleasure or as part of rituals, and they played ball games. They were primarily fishermen and hunters, although they did cultivate kitchen gardens and developed a system of shift cultivation, known as 'conuco'. They were also accomplished potters and weavers.

Above: Don Juan Beach Resort
Middle: Dorado Naco Beach Resort
Below: Punta Cana Beach Resort

Above: El Juncal
Below: Don Juan Beach Resort

Spanish conquest

The Caribs wore gold jewellery, and the first Spanish conquistadores quickly extracted the information about where to find it. This was one reason why Columbus founded the south coast settlement of Santo Domingo.

The Spanish showed their gratitude by enslaving the Indians and working them, often to death, in the gold and silver mines.

The Caribs on the island were grouped under five chieftains, the most powerful of whom was Bohechio, and when he died, his sister Anacaona took over. She was imprisoned as the Spanish steadily slaughtered her people, especially during 1503 in what became known as the Jaragua massacre. Despite the carnage, she wrote:

"Killing is not honourable, neither does violence redress an insult. Let us build a bridge of love that our enemies may cross, leaving their footprints for all to see."

Columbus was appointed Viceroy of all the Indies but spent much of his time exploring further west. His second voyage of discovery lasted from 1493-96, and his third voyage lasted from 1498 to 1500 when he was called home in disgrace because of his poor administration of the colonies, leaving his eldest son Diego in charge.

Diego's governorship was not officially sanctioned, however, and he returned to Spain after his father's death in 1506 to fight to have his position recognised by the crown. He was successful, and in 1508 was appointed Governor of the Indies.

In July, 1509 he arrived back in Santo Domingo and he remained Governor and Viceroy until his death in 1526.

He spent his time overseeing the expansion of the Spanish Empire in the New World, and it was from Santo Domingo that expeditions sailed under Cortez, Ponce de Leon and Velazquez, that were to acquire Mexico, Cuba and Puerto Rico for the Spanish crown.

Hispaniola, as the island came to be known, was the jewel in Spain's New World crown. Santo Domingo became the most prosperous city and capital of the fast-growing colonial empire. Magnificent buildings were constructed, and Santo Domingo boasts the first Cathedral, the first Monastery, the first University and the first Hospital built in the New World.

The old Colonial City on the banks of the River Ozama provided a clear insight into the wealth and importance of Santo Domingo during this time.

The early period of Spanish Colonial rule on Hispaniola, which served as a blueprint for settlement on other islands, was bloody and barbaric. The Caribs, who would not work for the Spanish, were killed or died of European diseases to which they had little resistance.

The Roman Catholic Church was as mighty as the conquistadores swords, and as harsh in its treatment of dissent. The Indians did not submit without a fight, and one of the country's great folk heroes is **Enriquillo**, a Taino chief, who waged a guerrilla war against the Spanish in the 1520s.

For the first half of the 16th century, Hispaniola's gold mines produced treasures which were sent back to Spain, while the fertile fields and ranches yielded crops and live meat for the expeditions and ships crews. As the Spanish explorations of the New World continued, however, Hispaniola's influence waned because of richer pickings elsewhere.

Although some Spanish settlers remained most left, and for the next 300 years or so, Hispaniola was left to its own devices. It was still a colony of Spain but received little investment or support, despite repeated attacks by pirates and British, Dutch and French privateers.

French occupation

The French, who had seized the western part of the island at the end of the 16th century, eventually had their claim recognised at the Treaty of Rijswijk (Ryswick) in 1697, which ended the War of the Grand Alliance in which France had faced the united might of England, Spain, Holland and the Holy Roman Empire.

The French part of the island was known as **Saint Domingue**, and planters were given land grants to establish sugar cane plantations which were worked by imported African slaves. Saint Domingue became fabulously wealthy because of "King Sugar", while the rest of the island struggled to survive.

The 19th century was a time of great upheaval with the island constantly fought over and frequently overrun by Spanish and Haitian forces. The people had to fight for their freedom many times during the century.

In 1791, Pierre-Dominique **Toussaint** l'Ouverture led Saint Domingue's 500,000 slaves in an uprising against the French colonial masters.

Above: El Seibo Church **Below:** Village hut, Enriquillo beach

Above: Santo Domingo Basilica
Right: The doorway to Higuey Basilica

Santo Domingo, always keen to attack its arch enemy France, sent Spanish troops to support the uprising. Toussaint, however, switched his allegiance back to France after the French Revolution in 1793, when the Government of the newly declared French Republic outlawed slavery throughout the colonies.

The Spanish force had to retreat back across the border, although the uprising continued. Most of the French settlers were killed or fled, and the fighting then degenerated into a bloody civil war between the slaves in the north and those in the south of Saint Domingue.

In 1801, the victorious Toussaint led a force into Spanish Hispaniola and quickly overran the country, meanwhile in Saint Domingue the freedom movement continued to gather momentum.

Napoleon Bonaparte sent troops led by his brother-in-law General Leclerc, to try to suppress the insurrection but they could not, and in 1804 Saint Domingue achieved independence and changed its name to **Haiti**.

Haitian invasion

The Haitians occupied the country until 1808 when the people finally rebelled against the oppression. The following year, with the aid of the British Royal Navy, they captured Santo Domingo, forced the Haitians back across the border, and declared themselves a republic.

Spain refused to accept this, and in 1814 re-established colonial rule. In 1821 the people rose up again and overthrew Spanish rule, but the following year, were invaded again by Haiti who occupied the country for 22 years.

The Haitian regime was run by **Jean-Pierre Boyer** who freed all slaves and did his best to break the power of the church and the traditional landowners and merchants, by closing the university and banning all European traditions.

During the 1830's La Trinitaria, the underground freedom movement, gathered momentum, led by Sanchez, Mella and **Juan Pable Duarte**, the father of Dominican Independence.

Boyer was himself the victim of a coup in Haiti in 1843, and the Dominicans, taking advantage of the resulting upheaval, rose up in 1844, attacked and defeated the Haitian occupying troops, and freed the country once again.

Padre Suntan, became

president of the new Dominican Republic, but he wasn't keen to have Duarte and the other freedom fighter leaders around, and he exiled them all.

Haiti proved a constant threat, however, and attacks across the border became so frequent that in 1861, Suntan petitioned Spain for the country to become a province of Spain with himself as Governor-General.

For four years the country was governed by Spain but there were frequent battles as freedom fighters fought with Spanish troops.

By 1865, Spain had had enough, recalled its soldiers and asked **President Ulysses S. Grant** to annex the colony as part of the United States. He recognised the island's strategic position on the seaways used by both American and European shipping bound for the Panama Canal, but the annexation plan was rejected by the U.S. Senate, because of a land speculation scandal, and for the next 18 years there was considerable disorder.

In 1882 **Ulises Heureaux** seized power and ruled as a dictator until 1899 when he was assassinated. Although his rule was harsh, he did introduce stability and for the first time in almost 300 years, there was a period of significant economic growth. He attracted foreign investment, built new roads and encouraged industrial development, but he did little to improve the conditions of the vast majority of the population who became even poorer. He was followed by a succession of leaders, including the **Archbishop Adolfo Nouel**, but none was able to restore law and order, and the economy plummeted.

American stewardship

In 1916 the continuing unrest had become so serious, that U.S. marines were sent in and they stayed until 1924 with U.S. officials administering the country.

During this period, the Americans did improve the infrastructure, building roads and schools, extending communications, and training a military-style constabulary to police the island. One of the men trained by the U.S. marines was a sergeant in the Dominican army, Rafael Leonides Trujillo Molina.

Trujillo was in control of the army, when a popular rebellion broke out in 1930. Rather than defend the government of Horacio Vasquez, he stood back and watched it topple and then declared himself president. He ruled the country with absolute power and great cruelty until 1961, when he too was assassinated.

The country under Trujillo was a repressive police state and political opponents simply disappeared. He even renamed the capital Ciudad Trujillo. Although the upper echelons of society prospered as he brought stability to the country and encouraged modernisation, there was appalling poverty and evidence of this still survives.

After his death, unrest broke out again, but in 1963 Juan **Bosch** came to power at the head of the Dominican Revolutionary Party, the first totally democratically-elected Government in the country's history. Within seven months though he was toppled, and the situation deteriorated so much that in 1965, U.S. marines were sent back to the island to help restore order after an uprising on 24 April. A ceasefire was ordered on 6 May and Hector Garciua-Godoy was declared provisional president.

After free elections held the following year installed Joaquin **Balaguer** as president, the peace-keeping force of 11,000 soldiers (9,000 from the U.S. and 2,000 from other OAS countries) was withdrawn.

In 1978 during elections for a fourth term in office, Balaguer called the army in to halt the counting of votes when it appeared he was trailing. After a warning from U.S. **President Jimmy Carter**, however, he backed down. Ballot boxes which had "disappeared" were returned, counting of the votes continued and Antonio **Guzmán** of the opposition Dominican Revolutionary Party (PRD) was declared President. Modest reforms were set back by the devastating effects of Hurricane David in 1979.

Guzmán was succeeded by Salvador Jorge **Blanco** of the DRP in 1982, who, on the advice of the International Monetary Fund, implemented a package of austerity measures. These led to serious rioting in the spring of 1984 which left more than 50 dead.

In 1986, **Balaguer** was re-elected President and he remained in power at the head of the Social Christian Reformist Party (PRSC) until 1996 when he stepped down, having served his maximum number of terms in office under the constitution.

Present day

On June 30, 1996, lawyer **Leonel Fernandez** was narrowly elected the country's new

Opposite page: *Higuey Basilica*

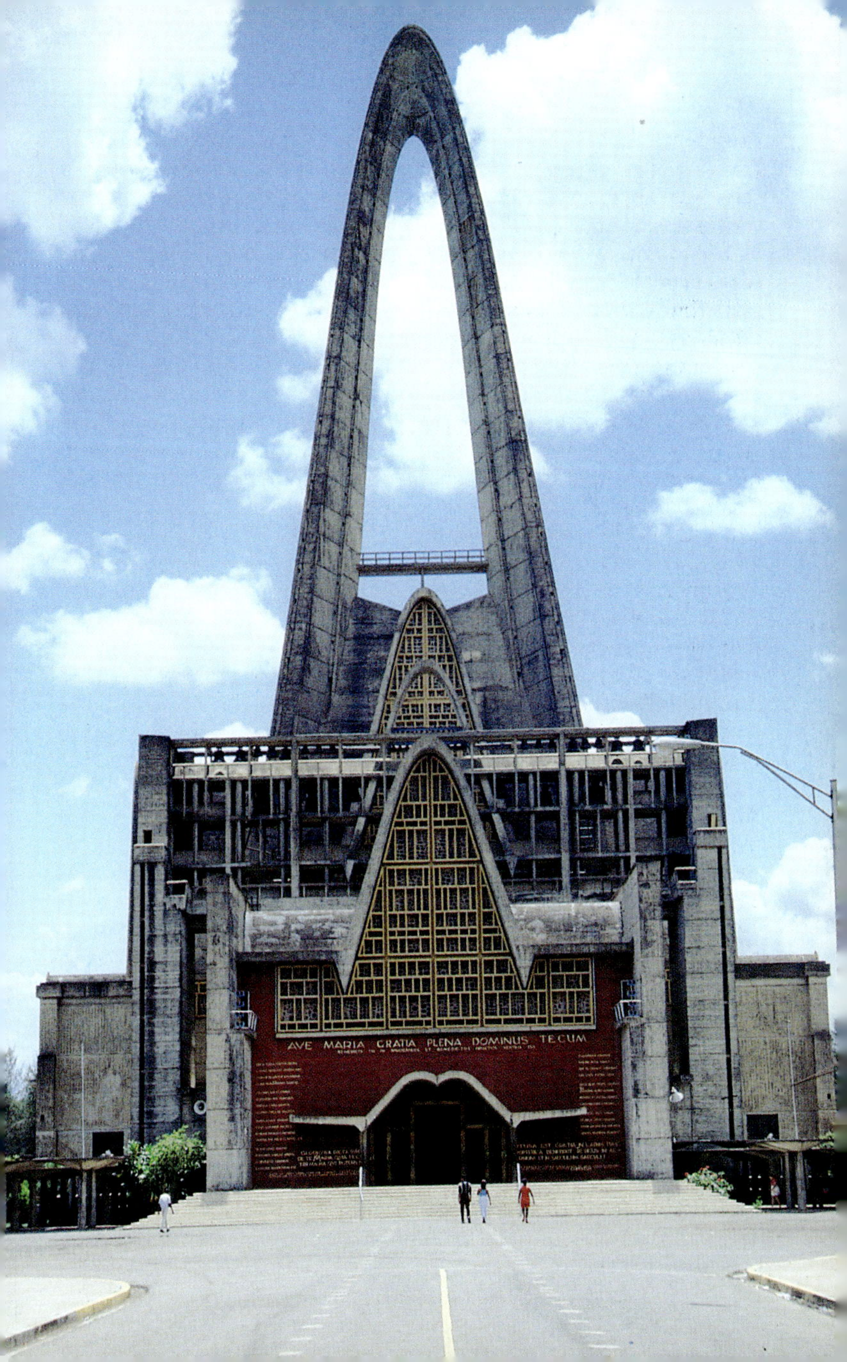
AVE MARIA GRATIA PLENA DOMINUS TECUM

President. Aged 42, he is the country's youngest President and the first from the Dominican Liberation Party.

Note: Caribbean politics often lead to very heated, and sometimes violent confrontations. As with Jamaica, it is prudent to keep a low profile or stay out of the cities during elections.

People

Most of the 7.8 million people are of African or mixed descent, although there are also European, Chinese, Japanese and many other races represented.

The first Africans were introduced in the 16th century to work alongside the Carib Indians in the gold mines, and then later to work on the plantations. Although the first settlers were Spanish, there was significant immigration during the 19th and 20th centuries from England, France, Germany and the Middle East. The Chinese established themselves mainly as shopkeepers, hoteliers and restauranteurs, while the Japanese farmed in the Constanza Valley.

Apart from the major towns and cities, there is a very scattered rural population. Regional settlement patterns tend to be around a main town, with some villages, but mainly sprawling, scattered small farming communities of a few houses and shacks (bohios) around a store or church. Many are very remote and can only be reached on foot or horseback.

About 40 per cent of the population still live in the country, but the exodus to urban areas continues. There has also been a substantial emigration to the United States over the past 30 years.

Many of the people who live in and around Azua near the south coast and the Bahia de Ocoa, are descended from immigrants who came from the Canary Islands, while European settlers largely occupied the south east grasslands where they raised cattle.

Most people live in and around the capital Santo Domingo (about 2 million), or in the Cibao Valley, which runs all the way from the Samaná Peninsula in the north east to Monte Cristi in the north west. The main population centres are Santo Domingo 2.2 million, Santiago 700,000, La Vega 180,000 and San Pedro de Macoris 140,000.

Religion

About 90 per cent of the population is Roman Catholic, and

there are Catholic, Evangelical and Seventh Day Adventist churches and synagogues. English services are held in the capital city.

Santeria

This African cult has gained enormous ground in the past few years and often goes hand in hand with Catholic worship in the more remote rural areas.

Santeria is founded on the belief that spirits exist in all things in nature, and that everything is pre-destined by a supreme God. Serving Him are several hundred other gods who act as intermediaries between God and the people.

Many of the original African deities now have the names of Catholic saints and it is not unusual to find Santeria shrines alongside Catholic shrines in some churches.

Santeros, or priests, have mystical powers that enable them to interpret the wishes of the gods, and each worshipper has his or her own 'patron saint'. These patron saint gods all have special powers, and are associated with special colours which their worshippers wear. Worship can include animal sacrifice, drumming, pulsating music and dancing, and the use of effigies: many worshippers often fall into trances because of the hypnotic rhythm of the drums.

Culture and Festivals

The culture today is a combination of Latin, Caribbean and African with other influences thrown into the melting pot.

Dominicans take their pleasures seriously, probably because of their ancestry and history of hard times. After sunset, they promenade to see and be seen; if there is music, and there always is, impromptu dancing often breaks out.

Music

Talented amateur musicians need little excuse to play, and music, song and dance are universally popular, not least because they are free.

The traditional rhythms of **merengue** and **bolero** now blend with modern pop music and the latest Latin beats. Merengue is the country's pulse, a beat that is impossible to ignore, and one that can persuade even the most shrinking violet to get up and move with the music.

The merengue is intrinsically Dominican and started in the mid 19th century, although it has now spread throughgout the Caribbean and much of Latin America. Every July, the

Merengue Festival is held in Santo Domingo, and it is a week-long non-stop party of music, dancing, dining and drinking.

Almost every small community has its own combo (band), usually consisting of drum (tambora), accordion and a guira, which traditionally was a gourd filled with stones or seeds, but can now be a washboard or cheese grater. The tambora has a very distinctive sound and it is claimed this is produced because the skin of an old male goat is stretched over one side of the drum, with the skin of a young female goat that has never had kids, over the other. Home-made instruments are easily made, such as flutes from bamboo cane and marimbas from seed pods.

Dancing

Dancing is the national passion, and even small communities have regular dances on Friday, Saturday and especially Sunday nights. Dominican young men still like to serenade their sweethearts after sunset, so don't be surprised if your sleep is disturbed by a love sick balladeer.

African customs and traditions are most evident in music and dance, which is popular everywhere. The Spanish and Middle East influences can also be heard in music and song, especially folk music.

Carnival

Carnival is the main festival of the year and takes place before Lent. The most colourful carnival is held in Santiago, and it lasts for many days with parades, Carnival Queen contest, displays of arts and crafts, and lots and lots of music.

The Dominicans celebrate a large number of national feast days, and every town and community has its own patron saint (fiesta patronal), the excuse for yet more festivities and partying.

Art and Literature

The country has produced many fine writers and poets, such as the 19th century Felix Maria del Monte, considered by many as the father of Dominican literature.

The struggle for freedom is a major feature of many works, especially the paintings of Manuel de Jesus Galvan, who used images of the early settlers' harsh treatment of the Caribs, to represent the repression felt by the Dominicans under continuing Spanish rule.

There are also many talented and internationally-acclaimed artists, sculptors, woodcarvers and weavers. Pottery and decorative ceramics are another

Above: El Seibo River **Below:** Altos de Chavón

expression of Domincana art, beuatifully fashioned by craftsmen such as Said Musa, Ignacio Ramiree, Néstor Palmer, Landy Lahoz, José Tiburcio and Teófilo Rosario Jimenénez.

There is also a national symphony orchestra and theatre, museums and art galleries.

Universities

The Autonomous University of Santo Domingo was founded in 1538 and is the oldest in the New World. It is independent although it receives government funding. The Pedro Henriquez Ureua National University in San Domingo, is supported by the Catholic Church and also receives government and private funding, as does the Madre Maestra Catholic University in Santiago. There is also the Central University of the East in San Pedro de Macoris, and the Santiago Technical University, both founded in the early 1970s.

Economy

Agriculture continues to be a mainstay of the economy, although there is a reasonably strong manufacturing base and tourism continues to grow in importance.

Since 1984 tourism has been the country's main industry and the most important foreign income earner. The country has more than 28,000 hotel rooms, more than any other Caribbean destination, and attracts about 2 million tourists a year.

Agriculture

Much of the country is fertile except in the far south west of Pedernales where the landscape is rocky. About one third of the land is under cultivation, even in high mountain valleys, and the country is largely self-sufficient in basic food stuffs. It also exports significant quanties of natural produce, especially raw sugar cane and molasses, but also tobacco, cocoa, coffee, rice, bananas and other tropical fruits, sorghum, tomatoes and root crops. Bagasse, the fibre left after the sugar cane juice has been extracted, is also exported as animal feed.

There has been a re-allocation of land in recent years to non-traditional crops both for the home and export markets. These include winter vegetables and fruits such as avocados, mangoes, papayas, passionfruit, bananas, pineapples, limes and strawberries.

Other crops include rice, corn, potatoes, tubers, beans, spices, peanuts, cashews, almonds, coconuts, plantains and citrus fruits.

Livestock is largely reared for the home market and the tourist industry. The savanna (grasslands) of the south east are on land that was once under the sea. The soil, fertile because of rich marine sedimentary deposits, was used for ranching but is now largely used to grow sugar cane. Rice is grown in the area around San Juan.

Although a tenth of the land area is covered in forest, timber is not a significant industry and neither is fishing, other than to satisfy home demand.

Minerals

Gold, silver, iron, nickel, gypsum, copper, marble and bauxite are mined commercially, although the Republic does have significant reserves of many other minerals, especially coal, sulphur, titanium, cobalt, tin, zinc and molybdenum.

The republic also has major reserves of **amber** and **larimar** which are used by local craftsman. Amber is not a stone, but the fossilised resin from trees millions of years old. It can vary in colour from almost clear to yellow, orange and red, and rare pieces, such as those containing sections of leaves, are very valuable.

Most of the island's amber comes from the mountains south of Puerto Plata, but some is mined close to El Valle in the south east and just outside Santo Domingo.

Larimar is a semi-precious stone, and only found in the Dominican Republic, which gives rise to its other name of **Dominican Turquoise**.

Industry

Oil has been located, but has not been exploited to any great extent.

Salt is produced in large quantities from Lake Enriquillo, and, to a lesser extent, from near Monte Cristi.

Many of the main industries are concentrated in **tax free zones** and these include clothing, textiles, shoes, electronic equipment, leather and sporting goods, furniture, pharmaceuticals, cement and concrete blocks and an oil refinery.

Major industries outside these zones are sugar production and food processing, plus local industries making items such as cigars, soap, candles and ropes.

Main exports are gold, silver, ferro-nickel, sugar, coffee, cocoa, tobacco, meats, fruits, vegetables, tourism and tax free industrial zone services.

Main imports are foodstuffs, petroleum and industrial raw materials.

The Government and Judiciary

The Government is a representative democracy. Presidential elections are held every four years, and legislative power is in the hands of the Congress consisting of the Senate and the Chamber of Deputies, also elected by popular vote every four years.

There are 30 provinces, each run by a Governor and its own civil government, plus the Capital District. Each province and district is represented in the Senate. Each province and the Capital District has two representatives in the Chamber of Deputies. Provinces are divided into municipalities that have their own councils.

Successive constitutions have, however, conferred enormous powers on the president in the event of an emergency, so that in effect the legislative assemblies can easily be overruled.

All citizens must vote if they are 18 or over, or earlier if they are married.

The main political parties are the Dominican Liberation Party (PLD), Reformist Social Christian Party (PRSC), Dominican Revolutionary Party (PRD), and the Independent Revolutionary Party (PRI), plus more than 20 other active minority parties.

The justice system is based on the Napoleonic Code with local courts handling both criminal and civil cases, and appeals going to the Supreme Court.

Food and drink

There is a huge choice when it comes to eating out, from excellent traditional island fare to the finest international cuisine at the best tourist hotels. There are lively ice cream parlours where you can find delicious, exotically flavoured treats, traditional Dominican restaurants and a wealth of ethnic styles from Argentinian to Italian, Peruvian to British, Swiss and Japanese. Always check before dining whether the restaurant accepts credit cards or only takes cash.

Dining out offers the chance to experiment with all sorts of unusual spices, vegetables and fruits, with creole and island dishes, not forgetting rum punches and other exotic cocktails.

Fruits and spices

There are so many exotic edible fruits and spices on the island that not all may be familiar to the visitor. For those who are interested, here is a list of the most popular ones, describing

Above: Altos de Chavón Amphitheatre   **Below**: El Juncal

their flavour and culinary uses:

Bananas are one of the Caribbean's most important exports (thus their nickname 'green gold') and they grow everywhere. Although they grow tall, bananas are not trees but herbaceous plants.

There are three types of banana plant: the first is the banana that we normally buy in supermarkets, which originated in Malaya and was introduced into the Caribbean in the early 16th century by the Spanish: the second is the large banana, or plantain, originally from southern India and the East Indies, and largely used in cooking – often fried and served as an accompaniment to fish and meat: the third variety is the red banana, which is not grown commercially, and is quite rare.

Most banana plantations cover only a few acres and are worked by the owner or tenant, although there are still some very large holdings. Bananas need a lot of attention, and island farmers will tell you that there are not enough hours in a day to do everything that needs to be done. The crop needs fertilising regularly, leaves need cutting back, and you will often see the fruit growing inside blue tinted plastic containers, which protect it from insect and bird attack, and speed up maturation.

Breadfruit

Breadfruit has large dark, green leaves, and the large green fruits can weigh 10-12lbs (4-5kg). The falling fruits explode with a loud bang and splatter its pulpy contents over a large distance. It is said that no one goes hungry when the breadfruit is in season. Breadfruit is a cheap carbohydrate-rich food, best eaten fried, baked or roasted over charcoal, because it is pretty tasteless when boiled. The tree was introduced to the Caribbean by Captain Bligh in 1793. The 1200 breadfruit saplings he brought from Tahiti aboard the *Providence*, were first planted in Jamaica and St. Vincent, and then quickly

A banana produces a crop about every nine months, and each cluster of flowers grows into a hand of bananas. A bunch can contain up to twenty hands of bananas, with each hand having up to 20 individual fruit. Once the plant has produced fruit, a shoot from the ground is cultivated to take its place, and the old plant dies.

Calabash trees are native to the Caribbean and have huge gourd like fruits which are very

spread throughout the islands.

Bligh's attempts to bring in young breadfruit trees may have been the reason for the mutiny on the *Bounty* four years earlier.

Bligh was given the command of the 215-ton *Bounty* in 1787 and was ordered to take the bread fruit trees from Tahiti to the West Indies where they were to be used to provide cheap food for the slaves.

The ship had collected its cargo and had reached Tonga when the crew under Fletcher Christian mutinied. The crew claimed that Bligh's regime was too tyrannical, and he and 18 members of the crew who stayed loyal to him, were cast adrift in an open boat. The cargo of breadfruit was dumped overboard. Bligh, in a remarkable feat of seamanship, navigated the boat for 3,600 miles (5796km) until making landfall on Timor in the East Indies.

Some authorities have claimed that it was the breadfruit tree cargo that sparked the mutiny, as each morning the hundreds of trees in their heavy containers had to be carried on deck, and then carried down into the hold at nightfall. It might have proved just too much for the already overworked crew.

The slaves did not like the breadfruit at first, but the plantings spread and the tree can now be found almost everywhere.

versatile when dried and cleaned. They can be used as water containers and bowls, bailers for boats, and as lanterns. Juice from the pulp is boiled into a concentrated syrup and used to treat coughs and colds and the fruit is said to have many other medicinal uses.

Cocoa is another important crop, and its Latin name *theobroma* means 'food of the gods'. A cocoa tree can produce several thousand flowers a year, but only a fraction of these will develop into seed bearing pods. It is the heavy orange pods that hang from the cocoa tree which contain the beans in which are the seeds that produce cocoa and chocolate.

The beans are split open; they contain a sweet white sap that protects the seeds and are kept in trays to ferment. This process takes up to eight days and the seeds must stay at a regular temperature to ensure the right flavour and aroma develops. The seeds are then dried.

In the old days, people used to walk barefoot over the beans to polish them and enhance their appearance. Today, the beans are crushed to extract cocoa butter, and the remaining powder is cocoa. Real chocolate is produced by mixing cocoa powder, cocoa butter and sugar.

In the markets you can sometimes buy cocoa balls which make a delicious drink. Each ball is the size of a large cherry. Simply dissolve the ball in a pan of boiling water, allow to simmer and then add sugar and milk or cream, for a rich chocolate drink. Each ball will make about four mugs of chocolate.

Coconut trees are incredibly hardy, and able to grow in sand even when regularly washed by salty sea water. They can also survive long periods without rain. Their huge leaves, up to 20 feet (6m) long in mature trees, drop down during dry spells so a smaller surface area is exposed to the sun which reduces evaporation.

Coconut palms can grow up to 80 feet (24m) tall, and produce up to 100 seeds a year. The seeds are the second largest in the plant kingdom, and these fall when ripe.

The coconut traditionally bought in greengrocers, is the seed with its layer of coconut surrounded by a hard shell. This shell is then surrounded by a layer of copra, a fibrous material, and this is covered by a large green husk. The seed and protective coverings can weigh 30lbs (13kg) and more. The seed and casing is waterproof, drought proof and able to float, and this explains why coconut palms which originated in the Pacific and Indian Oceans, are now found throughout the Car-

Coconut tales

Coconut palms are everywhere and should be treated with caution. Anyone who has heard the whoosh of a descending coconut and leapt to safety, knows how scary the sound is. Those who did not hear the whoosh, presumably did not live to tell the tale. Actually, very few people do get injured by falling coconuts and that is a near miracle in view of the tens of thousands of palms all over the island, but it is not a good idea to picnic in a coconut grove!

Above: Puerto Plata Fort   **Below**: Restaurant at Altos de Chavón

ibbean – the seeds literally floated across the seas.

The coconut palm is extremely versatile. The leaves can be used as thatch for roofing, or cut into strips and woven into mats and baskets, while the husks yield coir, a fibre resistant to salt water and ideal for ropes, brushes and brooms.

Green coconuts contain a delicious thirst-quenching 'milk', and the coconut 'meat' can be eaten raw, or baked in ovens for two days before being sent to processing plants where the oil is extracted. Coconut oil is used in cooking, soaps, synthetic rubber and even in hydraulic brake fluid.

Whilst driving around the island, groups of men and women may be seen splitting the coconuts in half with machetes and preparing them for the ovens. You might also see halved coconut shells spaced out on the corrugated tin roofs of some homes. These are drying before being sold to the copra processing plants.

Dasheen (with its 'elephant ear' leaves), is one of the crops known as 'ground provisions' in the Caribbean, the others being sweet potatoes, yams, eddo and tannia. The last two are close relatives of dasheen, and all are members of the aroid family, one of the world's oldest cultivated crops.

Dasheen and eddo grow from a corm which, when boiled thoroughly, can be used like potato. The young leaves of both are used to make calaloo, a spinach-like soup (also spelled callaloo, kallaloo and several others ways). Both dasheen and eddo are thought to have come from China or Japan, but tannia is native to the Caribbean, and its roots can be boiled, baked or fried.

Guava is common throughout the West Indies, and the aromatic, sweet pink pulpy fruit is also a favourite with birds who then distribute its seeds. The fruit bearing shrub can be seen on roadsides and in gardens, and it is used to make a wide range of products from jelly to 'cheese', a paste made by mixing the fruit with sugar.

The fruit ranges in size from a golf ball to a tennis ball, is a rich source of vitamin A and contains lots more vitamin C than citrus fruit. Because it contains a lot of small seeds, it is best eaten as a jelly or as a flavoured ice-cream, or drunk as juice.

Guava juice is used as an ingredient in a number of tempting cocktails, but shouldn't be confused with the guavaberry, which also grows locally. The berries from this plant have been traditionally used by islanders to brew a special liqueur.

Mango can be delicious if somewhat messy to eat. Originally from India and the East Indies, it is now grown throughout the Caribbean and found wherever there are people. Young mangoes can be stringy and unappetising, but ripe fruit from mature trees which grow up to 50 feet (15m) and more, is usually delicious, and can be eaten raw or cooked. The juice is a great reviver in the morning, and the fruit is often used to make jams and other preserves, and great ice cream. The wood of the mango is often used by boatbuilders.

Passion fruit is not widely grown but it can usually be bought at the market. The pulpy fruit contains hundreds of tiny seeds, and many people prefer to press the fruit and drink the juice. It is also commonly used in fruit salads, sherbets and ice creams.

Pawpaw or papaya trees are also found throughout the islands and are commonly grown in gardens. The trees are prolific fruit producers but grow so quickly that the fruit soon becomes difficult to gather.

The large, juicy melon-like fruits are eaten fresh, pulped for juice or used locally to make jams, preserves and ice cream. They are rich sources of vitamin A and C. The leaves and fruit contain an enzyme which tenderises meat and tough joints cooked wrapped in pawpaw leaves or covered in slices of fruit, usually taste like much more expensive cuts.

Nutmeg

Nutmeg trees are found on all the Caribbean islands. The tree thrives in hilly, wet areas and the fruit is the size of a small tomato. The outer husk, which splits open while still on the tree, is used to make the very popular nutmeg jelly. Inside, the seed is protected by a bright red casing which when dried and crushed, produces the spice mace. Finally, the dark outer shell of the seed is broken open to reveal the nutmeg which is dried and then ground into a powder, or sold whole so that it can be grated to add flavour to dishes.

The same enzyme, papain, is also used in chewing gum, cosmetics, the tanning industry and, somehow, in making wool shrink-resistant. A tea made from unripe fruit is said to be good for lowering high blood pressure. Ripe papaya slices and lime make a delicious, healthy breakfast.

Pigeon Peas are widely cultivated and can be found in many

Above: Casa de Bastidas   **Below**: Alcazar

Above: Santo Cerro Church **Below**: La Romana Pottery

vated and can be found in many back gardens. The plants are very hardy and drought resistant, and give prolific yields of peas which can be eaten fresh or dried and used in soups and stews.

Pineapples were certainly grown in the Caribbean by the time Columbus arrived, and were probably brought from South America by the Amerindians. The fruit is slightly smaller than the Pacific pineapple, but the flavour is more intense. Most fruit for export destined for our supermarkets, is picked before it is ripe so that it arrives many days later in reasonable condition. Really ripe fruit straight from the tree has a much more intense aroma, bursts with juice and flavour, and has almost no core, as this only develops as it ages.

Soursop is a member of the same family as the sugar apple and can be seen growing in hedgerows and gardens. Its spikey, pulpy fruits have lots of little black seeds inside. They are eaten fresh, or used for preserves, drinks and ice cream.

Sugar Apple is a member of the annona fruit family, and grows wild and in gardens throughout the islands. It is also called the custard apple and sweetsop, because it is a lot sweeter than the soursop. The small, soft sugar apple fruit can be peeled off in strips when ripe, and is like eating thick apple sauce. It can be eaten fresh or used to make sherbet or drinks.

Plantain

Plantain is another import from the East Indies, not to be confused with its cousin, the smaller yellow banana. Plantains are bigger, more versatile and a staple part of the Caribbean diet, and must always be cooked before eating. One way of identifying bananas and plantains on the tree, is that banana fingers on the hand generally point upwards, while plantain fingers normally point downwards – or so I am assured.

Sugar Cane is still grown commercially but is less important than it was. Most of the cane is grown to produce molasses for the rum industry. The canes can grow up to 12 feet (4m) tall and after cutting, are crushed to extract the sugary juice. The juice is then boiled until the sugar crystalises out and the remaining mixture is molasses, used to produce rum.

The **Tamarind** originally came from India, but is now a

common sight throughout the Caribbean. The trees can grow very tall and bushy, and are long living, with dangling bulbous pods, that contain the rather tart fruit. The edible part is the pulp that surrounds the seeds, and it makes a delicious drink, and is also often added to curries and seasonings. It is also one of the special ingredients in Lea and Perrins Worcestershire sauce which makes it so distinctive. It is even said that the pulp can be used to bring back the shine to tarnished brass and copper.

Quite often the area around the base of tamarind is devoid of other vegetation, because the tree's roots give out a toxic chemical which kills off other plants – a remarkable self-defence mechanism to help it survive in places where nutrients may be at a premium.

Restaurants

Eating out is very relaxed and few restaurants have a strict dress code, although most people like to wear something a little smarter at dinner after a day on the beach or out sightseeing. Many hotels have a tendency to offer buffet dinners or barbecues, but even these can be interesting and tasty affairs.

Breakfast

Breakfast can be one of the most exciting meals of the day for a visitor. There is a huge range of freshly squeezed fruit juices to choose from. Try a glass of water melon juice, followed by a fresh grapefruit, or slices of chilled paw-paw or mango. Most hotels provide fruit plates offering a wide choice, so you should be able to taste your way through them all during your stay.

The island's fruits also make great jams and preserves, and you can follow the fruit with piping hot toast spread with perhaps citrus marmalade or guava jam, and finish off with a delicious cup of the island's own coffee.

Most tourist hotels also offer traditional American breakfasts for those who can't do without them.

During the summer, there are fruits such as the kenip, plumrose, sugar apple and yellow plum. Green bananas and plantains are usually eaten raw, or boiled or steamed in the skin, then cut into slices and served very hot. They also make excellent chips when fried.

Lunch and dinner

Lunch and dinner menus usually offer a similarly good choice.

Starters include a huge choice of fruit juices from orange and grapefruit to the more unusual ones like soursop and tamarind. Green coconut 'milk' is also very thirst quenching. Traditional Caribbean starters also include dishes such as Christophene and coconut soup.

Callaloo soup is made throughout the Caribbean from the spinach-like young leaves of dasheen or eddo; ochroes, smoked meat and sometimes crab can be added, as well as lots of herbs and spices.

Chicken strips (chicharrones) with a spicy dip marinated green bananas and fish and chowders are also popular appetisers.

Try heart of palm, excellent fresh shrimps or scallops, smoked kingfish wrapped in crepes or crab backs, succulent land crab meat sautéed with breadcrumbs and seasoning, and served re-stuffed in the shell. It is much sweeter than the meat of sea crabs. The crabs from Puerto Plata and Miches are especially good.

Fish

The fish is generally excellent, and don't be alarmed if you see dolphin on the menu. It is not the protected species made famous by 'Flipper', but a solid, close-textured flat faced fish called the dorado, which is delicious. Salt fish often appears on the menu. Salting was the most common form of food preserving, and allowed surplus catches to be safely kept until times of food shortage, or for when the seas were too rough for the fishing boats to go to sea.

There is also snapper, grouper, kingfish, redfish, jacks, balaouy, snapper, tuna, flying fish, lobster, swordfish, baby squid and mussels. There are delicious river crayfish and langostinos which are the larger saltwater variety, mussels and oyster.

Try locrio (paella) or a sort of seafood jambalaya with chunks of lobster and shrimps served on a bed of braised seasoned rice; shrimp creole, with fresh

---

Conch Shells

Conch shells are cleaned and sold to tourists but they have played an important role in country life for centuries. The Dominicans blow the shells as horns to announce news, both good and bad. In the countryside butchers will often give a blast on their conch shell 'trumpets' to announce supplies of freshly slaughtered meat, while the blowing of three low notes broadcasts the news that someone has died or is seriously ill.

shrimp sautéed in garlic butter and parsley and served with tomatoes, or fish creole, with fresh fish steaks cooked in a spicy onion, garlic and tomato sauce and served with rice and fried plantain. In Samaná in particular, you should try pescado con coco, which is fish simmered in a coconut sauce. Conch (pronounced conk) is very popular and served in many ways – as fritters, in soup and salads, and as a main course.

Vegetables

Vegetables most usually served with meals are plantains, rice, beans and root vegetables. Mangú, is mashed plantain, and is often prepared with lots of garlic and other herbs. It is frequently served at breakfast time, and has a reputation for being excellent for settling upset stomachs. Fritos verdes is fried green plantain.

For vegetarians there are excellent salads, stuffed breadfruit, callaloo bake, stuffed squash and pawpaw, baked sweet potato and yam casserole.

Stews

Stews are traditional Dominican fare because meals could be left to simmer for hours in the stew pot while the family was out working in the fields. Stews could also be used to provide tasty nourishing meals even for the poorest families, using the most basic ingredients.

Many main courses still involve hearty stews such as **sancocho**, the national dish, which can include many different types of meat, and is packed with vegetables and herbs; mondongo, a stew made with tripe and vegetables is also popular. There is sancocho prieto (black stew) which traditionally contains seven different meats, and carne guisada

Pepper Sauce

Another note of warning: on most tables you will find a bottle of pepper sauce. It usually contains a blend of several types of hot pepper, spices and vinegar, and should be treated cautiously. Try a little first before splashing it all over your food, as these sauces range from hot to unbearable.

If you want to make your own hot pepper sauce, take four ripe hot peppers, one teaspoon each of oil, ketchup and vinegar and a pinch of salt, blend together into a liquid, and bottle.

(beef stew). You will also find la bandera on the menu, which is a dish of white rice, red beans and stewed meat. The dish was given its name, which means 'the banner', because the ingredients have the same colours as the national flag.

Other island specialities include arroz con pollo, chicken with rice, usually served with fried plantains, chicharrones de pollo (special fried chicken) and delicious lechôn asado, roast suckling pig cooked on a spit. Moro, which is rice n' beans is virtually the national dish. Goat meat is delicious, especially in Azua and Monte Cristi, where the animals are fed on wild oregano, which gives the meat a wonderful flavour. Longaniza is a delicious spicy pork sausage, and morcilla is a rich black sausage.

On the buffet table, you will often see a dish called the pepper pot. This is usually a hot, spicy meat and vegetable stew to which may be added small flour dumplings and shrimps.

Island fast food also includes fritters and patties, spicy sausage and johnny cakes, which have been imported from the Leeward and Windward Islands.

Desserts

Desserts are often based on fruits and juices. Try fresh fruit salad, with added cherry juice, and sometimes a little rum, which is a year round favourite. There is a wide variety of fruit sherbets and refreshing milk shakes using tropical fruits such as soursop and tamarind. Exotically flavoured ice-creams are also delicious.

Because the country is a major sugar producer, there is a large range of candies and sweet desserts. There is dulce de leche, a sweet made from milk, dulce de coco which is made from coconut, and dulce de batata, a sweet potato candy, and even dulce de tomate, a sweet preserve made from tomatoes.

Other delicacies are banana fritters and banana flambé, coconut cheesecake, and green papaya or guava shells simmered in heavy syrup.

Breads

Breads are wonderful, and you should try them if you get the chance. Casabe is manioc bread, and catibias are manioc fritters; the recipes for both have been handed down since Taino times. There are also garlic, banana and pumpkin breads, and delicious cakes such as coconut loaf cake, guava jelly cookies and rum cake.

Some popular recipes

Sancocho – the national dish – serves 8 to 10.

(The recipe has been slightly altered as some of the original ingredients are not always readily available elsewhere).

Ingredients: A 2lb (0.9kg) chicken cut into pieces, 3 lbs fresh pork chops trimmed of fat and cut into pieces, 4 tablespoons of oil, 3 green plantains, 1 lb of yam, 1 lb of potatoes, 3 ears of corn, halved, 1 green pepper chopped, 1 large onion sliced, 3 coriander leaves, half a teaspoon of oregano, 3 cloves of garlic crushed, one quarter of a teaspoon of all-spice and two tablespoons of vinegar.

(For vinegar, Dominicans use agrio, the squeezed juice from the naranja agria, an orange with a pitted surface, which is poured over marble-sized onions, green pepper and garlic and left to mature for a week or so).

* Do not use ham or smoked pork and allow half a pound of meat per person. The original recipe also includes 1lb (0.5kg) of mapuey, half a pound each of white yautia and yellow yautia, half a pound of auyama, and 3 sprigs of cilantrico, but these may be difficult to find and can either be omitted, or you can experiment by adding extra yam and potatoes, or anything else you wish.

Preparation: Marinate the meat for two hours with the pepper, onion, coriander, oregano, garlic, all-spice and vinegar, then sauté the meat in oil in a large pot. Peel and dice the other vegetables and add to the meat, add water to cover and cook until the broth thickens. Add salt to taste.

Serve from the pot and spoon two spoons of cooked rice on top of each bowl of stew.

Chucharrones de Pollo (fried chicken).

If sancocho is the national dish, then this Dominican-style fried chicken is a close second.

Ingredients: 1 3-4lb (1.3-1.8kg) chicken, 2 tablespoons of Worcestershire or thick soy sauce, 3 tablespoons of lime juice, three quarters of a cup of flour, half a teaspoon of paprika, 2 green limes cut into pieces, half a cup of cooking oil, and one teaspoon of salt.

Preparation: Cut the chicken into pieces and wash. Cut the wings into two pieces, the breast into four and the drumsticks into two. Season the pieces with lime juice, Worcestershire sauce and salt, and set aside.

Rum

Rum has such fortifying powers that General George Wasington insisted every soldier be given a daily tot, and the daily ration also became a tradition in the British Royal Navy, lasting from the 18th century untill 1970.

Rum can be produced in two ways. It can be distilled directly from the fermented juice of crushed sugar cane, or made from molasses left after sugar, extracted from the cane by crushing, is boiled until it crystallies. Dark rums need extensive ageing in oak barrels, sometimes for up to 15 years, while light rums are more light bodied and require less ageing.

Columbus is credited with planting the first sugar cane in the Caribbean, on Hispaniola, during his third voyage, The Spanish called the drink produced from it aguardiente de cana, although it was officially named as saccharum, from the Latin name for sugar cane. It was English sailors who abbreviated this name to rum.

It is sometimes suggested that the word rum comes from an abbreviation of the word 'rumbullion'. While the origin of this word is unknown there is a record of it in 1672, and it was later used to describe a drunken brawl.

The first West Indian rum was produced in the Danish Virgin Islands in the 1660s and by the end of the century, there were thousands of distilleries throughout the Caribbean.

Rum rapidly became an important commodity and figured prominently in the infamous Triangle Trade in which slaves from Africa were sold for rum in the West Indies which was sold to raise money to buy more slaves.

Opposite Page: *Juan Dolio*

Mix the flour with salt and paprika, and roll each piece of chicken in the flour thoroughly twice. Heat the oil until a drop of water dropped into it pops, and fry the pieces until golden brown. Drain on paper towels and serve decorated with lime pieces.

Pescado con coco (fish with coconut). Serves four

Ingredients: 2 lbs (0.9kg) of red snapper, pollock or similar, half a teaspoon of pepper, 2 onions, 1 large pepper diced and cleaned of seeds, fresh greens, leek and parsley to taste, 4 or 5 limes, half a can of tomato sauce, 1 fresh coconut* or coconut milk substitute, 3 cloves of garlic and 2 to 3 tablespoons of cooking oil.

Preparation: Clean fish well and slice open. Squeeze the lime juice over the fish and rub in. Combine all seasonings, greens, garlic, onions and peppers in a blender and chop well. Use half of this mixture to season the open fish. Heat oil in a large pot, add the other half of the seasoning from the blender with tomato sauce and the coconut milk. Stir constantly to prevent lumps until the mixture boils. Place the open fish in the same pot and cook for 15 minutes, taking care that it does not break into pieces. Serve on a platter on a bed of lettuce and tomatoes.

* To get the milk from a fresh coconut, grate the white meat, add one cup of water and place in a clean cloth. Squeeze until all the liquid comes from the cloth.

Dulce de Coco (Coconut Fudge)

Ingredients: 1 large coconut, one and a half pounds (0.7kg) of sugar, one and half quarts of fresh milk, 1 piece of cinnamon, the rind of one lime, 1 cup of water and several clean glass jars with tight lids.

Preparation: Clean the coconut of its brown shell and clean well. Grate and add one cup of water. Set to boil adding sugar and cinamon, all the milk and lime rind. Cook for one and a half hours on a low flame stirring regulary. When the mixture is gooey and comes up clean from the bottom of the pan, the candy is ready. Leave to cool and then fill the jars and refrigerate. Serve chilled.

Drinks

Rum is the Caribbean drink. There are almost as many rums in the West Indies as there are malt whiskies in Scotland, and there is an amazing variety of strength, colour and quality.

The Dominican Republic still produces its own rum continuing a tradition more than 300 years old. Most of the production is for white rum, and there are some excellent barrel-aged drinks which are best sipped and enjoyed as liqueurs.

Mix your own cocktails

The **Painkiller** is a rum cocktail containing orange and pineapple juice, cream of coconut and a sprinkling of nutmeg.

There are scores of different rum cocktails, and here is one of the most popular.

Traditional Caribbean Plantation Rum Punch

To make Plantation Rum Punch, thoroughly mix 3 ounces of rum, with one ounce of lime juice and one teaspoon of honey, then pour over crushed ice, and for a little zest, add a pinch of freshly grated nutmeg.

Planter's Punch

Another favourite is **Planter's Punch,** which is made by combining 2 ounces each of pineapple juice, rum, cream of coconut and half an ounce of lime in a blender for one minute. Pour into a chilled glass, add a sprinkle of grated coconut and garnish with a slice of cherry and a slice of orange.

Hotels

Most tourist hotels and bars also offer a wide range of cocktails both alcoholic, usually very strong, and non-alcoholic. Tap water in hotels and resorts is generally safe to drink and mineral and bottled water is widely available, as are soft drinks.

There are also many very good island-brewed beers such as the light Presidente, and the darker, stronger Quisqueya.

Restaurants

While many of the main tourist hotel restaurants offer excellent service, time does not have the same urgency as it does back home, and why should it after all, as you are on holiday. Relax, enjoy a drink, the company and the surroundings and don't worry if things take longer – the wait is generally worth it.

3 LA CAPITAL: SANTO DOMINGO

Location

La Capital, as it is known, sits on the south coast and is the oldest city in the New World. It was here that Columbus ruled as Viceroy of the Indies, and from here that conquistadores such as Ponce de Leon, Cortez and Valezquez set sail to expand the Spanish New World empire.

The splendour of the original Colonial City can still be admired along the west bank of the Rio Ozama. Further west is the tourist strip and university and inland is busy central Santo Domingo with its crowded streets, walkways, offices and shops, as well as museums, parks, botanical gardens and a zoo.

Santo Domingo is not only the country's oldest city but by far the largest, covering an area of 144 square miles

(375sq.km). It is a city that buzzes by day and really comes to life at night with its nightclubs, bars, discos and casinos. There is the Malecón and Avenida del Puerto, that run along the seaside and never seem to sleep. There is the new open-air Teatro Agua Luz with its dancing waters, and the sensational Guácara Taina, set in a huge cavern, which stages folk dancing during the day and vibrates to the music and feet of thousands of disco dancers at night.

The city is surrounded by sprawling suburbs of wide avenues and expensive villas and homes, and beyond these are the shanty towns, which accommodate almost a third of the country's population.

Getting around

The best way to get round the centre of the city is on foot, but for outlying districts there are taxis and buses. The more adventurous can even ride pillion on a motorbike, be pulled round in a rickshaw, or ride in style in a horse and carriage.

History

The old city was founded by Columbus towards the end of his second voyage of discovery

Opposite: Santo Domingo courtyard

on 4 August 1496, and his brother Don Bartholomew was the first Governor. The settlement grew rapidly as people flooded in, attracted by the prospect of untold wealth in gold and silver on Hispaniola. The boom lasted for little more than half a century, but during that time money was lavished on the capital. Magnificent buildings were erected, parks were created and forts built to protect it. The first hospital, the first university and the first cathedral in the Americas, were all built during this period in Santo Domingo.

Dominican monks, headed by Fray Pedro de Córdoba, established a chapter in Santo Domingo in 1510 and then petitioned the Pope for permission to open a college. On 28 October 1538 the Santo Tomás de Aquino college opened, and is still functioning today as the Autonomous University of Santo Domingo.

The colonial city has been proclaimed by UNESCO as, "the city of cultural heritage of the New World."

The bubble burst in the middle of the 16th century as Hispaniola's wealth paled in comparison to the new found riches on Cuba, Puerto Rico and the mainland of Mexico and Florida. Many of Santo

Domingo's settlers, merchants and adventurers moved to these new colonies, and the capital started its slow decline.

In 1562 a massive earthquake hit the town and most of the original buildings were destroyed, leaving only those built of stone. The oldest building is Casa del Cordon which dates from 1503, but there are scores of wonderful old buildings, many of which have been well restored, and a walk around the Colonial City is a must. Most of these historic buildings now house cultural centres, art galleries, restaurants, boutiques and museums, and most can be visited free of charge.

The Colonial City - a walking tour

The Colonial City is built in a grid system with streets running parallel or at right angles to each other. They are clearly signposted to make it easy to get around and, if you are interested in antiquity and historic buildings, you need to set aside as much time as possible for your explorations.

Parque Independencia

Parque Independencia is a good place to start because it separates the Colonial City from new Santo Domingo. Carved into the stone pavement in the park is the Nautical Rose. This is the point from which all island distances are measured, so when you see a kilometre sign in the country that is how far it is from Independence Park and the Nautical Rose which marks Kilometer 0.

The park is close to the tourist strip around Avenida Independencia and Avenida George Washington which runs parallel with it along the waterfront.

Avenida El Conde is a broad pedestrian precinct, running for almost 900 yards (800m) in a straight line from Independence Park to the sea, and is the oldest shopping centre in the city. During the day it bustles with people shopping in the many fine stores, and in the evening it is almost as busy with people taking the night air and eating in the many restaurants and cafes.

The Colonial City used to be surrounded by a defensive wall and the **Puerto del Conde** is one of the original gateways into the city. The park contains the mausoleum built in 1976 in honour of Sanchez, Mella and Duarte, the Founding Fathers of Dominican independence. Under the Gate of El Conde burns an eternal flame in memory of the country's national heroes.

Fuerte de la Concepcion, the remains of a fort built in the 17th century, is to be found close to the north eastern corner of the park. Next to the fort is **Casa de Bastidas**, a complex of museums, galleries and shops.

Towards the river

From the fort take Avenida Las Mercedes and then turn left into Avenida Santome with **Inglesia San Lazaro** on your left: continue to Avenida Mella and turn right for **Mercado Modelo**. Continue east along Avenida Mella which runs almost all the way to the river mouth which is protected by **Fuerte de Santa Barbara** built around 1528.

South of the fort is the **Church of Santa Barbara**, and next to the church is the quarry from which almost all the colonial city buildings were constructed, and from where the material for the city wall was excavated in 1574.

St. Francis Monastery

Continue south, and then turn right into Avenida Vincente Celestino Duarte for **Ermita de San Anton** and the ruins of St. Francis Monastery. The Franciscan order was founded here in 1505, and the monastery was built between 1512 and 1514. It was the first church and monastery in the New World until Sir Francis Drake burned it to the ground during his raid in 1586. Guarocuya, who was baptised a Christian at the monastery and changed his name to Enriquillo, was educated there. The ruins are regularly used as the stage for cultural events.

Casa del Cordon

Casa del Cordon is the oldest building on the island. To find it, retrace your route and then turn right into Avenida Isabela La Catolica. Casa del Cordon is on the corner with Calle Emiliano Tejera. It was built in 1503 and is named after the braided cord worn by Franciscan monks round their habits. The building is now occupied by a branch of Banco Popular, but in the stone lintel above the main door, you can still see the original carving depicting a piece of cord. The bank allows people in to view the interior during normal banking hours.

Head east along Calle Emiliano Tejera to La Atarazana, and the magnificent Alcazar de Colon.

The Alcazar de Colon

The Alcazar de Colon was built between 1509 and 1512 by Diego Columbus, eldest son of Christopher. Work started the

SANTO DOMINGO

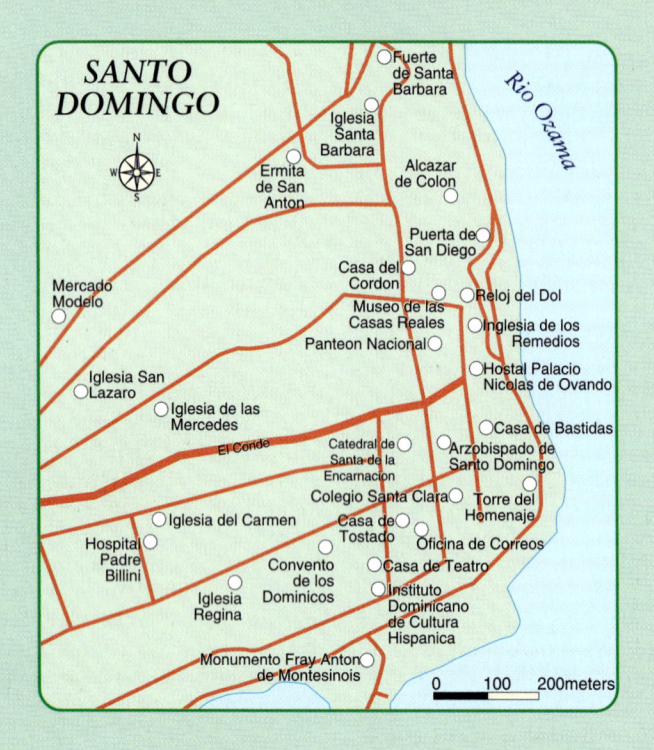

year after he arrived as the first Viceroy in the New World, a post he held until his death in 1526.

The palace was built from local coral stone on a rise overlooking the Ozama River for his court and Maria de Toledo, his wife. Spanish architects controlled 1,500 Indian builders who used only saws, chisels and hammers in the construction. Not a single nail was used in the 22 room building which combines Spanish, Gothic, Moorish and Italian Renaissance styles. The 72 doors and windows all pivot on mahogany bolts set into the thick walls.

Diego's two daughters Juana and Isabel were born there, and Indian chief Enriquillo and Mencia were married in the chapel in 1517. Two years later Enriquillo, who had been wronged by the Spanish authorities, led a rebellion against the Spanish which was to last 14 years until the Spanish sued for peace.

Restoration work started in the mid 1950s, and the original quarries were re-opened so that matching stone could be used. The two-storey building with its ornate arches and courtyards has been well restored and contains furniture and furnishings from the 16th and 17th centuries, including some wonderful tapestries.

Next door is the **Alcazar Museum** which displays religious and colonial works of art. Of interest on the southern facade is the Royal coat of arms of Queen Juana de Castilla, also known as Juana the Mad, because it is said that when her husband Philip the Handsome died she became insane. This is the only coat of arms of the queen known to exist anywhere in the world. The palace is open daily except Tuesday, between 9am and 6pm. There is a small admission charge.

La Atarazana

La Atarazana (Dockyard), the original commercial heart of the colonial city, is across the park from the fort and is a crescent of elegant official buildings and houses dating from the 16th century. Historically they contained the armoury and customs house with very grand warehouses alongside, but today they house duty-free shops, restaurants and bars to relax in over a drink, and a museum, which is open Monday to Saturday from 9am to 5pm and from 1-5pm on Sunday (☎ 682-5834).

The **Museum of Marine Archaeology** contains a fascinating collection of artifacts salvaged from the many ships that have foundered on the reefs around the island, including the *Concepsion*, the *Guadeloupe* and the *Tolosa*. There is also a display depicting what it was like to work as a deck hand aboard a 17th century galleon, a must for anyone who may have thought a life on the open seas would have been fun! The museum is open daily from 9am to 5pm, and there is a small admission charge.

The river is being dredged to accommodate cruise ships at the new cruise dock alongside the Colonial City, and close by the point where Columbus tied up his ships. The tree he used to tie up to has long since gone, but the spot is now marked by a symbolic concrete 'tree'. On the eastern side of the Ozama River are the remains of the Rosary Chapel, the oldest church on the island and dating from 1496.

The **Puerta de San Diego** is another of the original gates from the old colonial city walls, and was built in the 1540s.

Along the riverbank

Continue south along Avenida del Puerto to the **Museo de las Casas Reales**, on the Calle Las Damas. It was formerly the palace occupied by the Captain General and the offices of the colonial government, and it now contains a priceless collection of Spanish Colonial treasures, including many items salvaged from shipwrecked galleons, and 16th century art, furniture and weaponry. There are also displays depicting the different voyages of exploration by Columbus. It is open daily between 9am and 5pm except Monday (☎ 682-4202).

Inglesia de los Remedios is close by, a restored brick chapel dating from the 16th century, which predates the cathedral and was originally the private chapel of the Dávilas family. Beside it is the famous **Sundial** built by Governor Francisco Rubio y Peuaranda in 1758, which still indicates the time to passers by.

Panteon Naçional

Panteon Naçional with its eternal flame is opposite, standing as a monument to the heroes who fought in the struggle for independence over the years. The building was built as the monastery church for the Jesuit Order housed next door, and dates from 1714, although construction continued for another 40 years. It was restored by Trujillo between 1955 and 1958 as a memorial to the nation's heroes. The monument houses the remains of many of these heroes, including General Pedro Santana and patriot Maria Trinidad Sanchez, who was executed on the General's orders.

The central nave and the chapels running off it form a cross, and hanging from the dome is a huge bronze chandelier which was a gift to Trujillo from General Franco.

Architecture

The House of Jesuits is next to the Panteon, one of the oldest buildings in the Colonial City. It was built on the orders of Fray Nicolás de Ovando in 1511, and was the home of the Jesuits and the seat of Gorjón University. The complex is built around a large courtyard and includes the Casa de Villoria and the Casa de Gargoyles.

The Hostal Palacio Nicolas de Ovando was the home of Governor Nicolás Ovando, and the wealthy Dávilas family. It has been restored to its 16th century glory and is now a charming hotel with lovely inner courtyards, and balconies overlooking the Andalusian fountains. The building is of huge architectural importance because it is the only one in the Americas with a Gothic-Elizabethan portal.

Parque Colon

Parque Colon, named after Columbus, is south of El Conde. A statue of the great explorer stands looking out to the sea, and the park is surrounded by stone town houses and shaded arched walkways.

Palacio de Borgella on Parque Colon, was built during the 22 years of Haitian occupation from 1822, and later served as the home of the Dominican Congress until 1947 when it moved to the Palaçio National.

The Catedral de Santa Maria de la Encarnación

The Catedral de Santa Maria de la Encarnación is to the south, the first cathedral built in the New World. Although the corner stone was laid in 1510, work quickly ground to a halt when the architect Alonso Rodriquez sailed for Mexico to construct the cathedral in Mexico City. Work started again in 1521 and the cathedral was consecrated in 1540.

Although it has been added to over the years, it has survived hurricanes and earthquakes, a fitting tribute to the 16th century stone masons. The many additions also account for the rather unusual mix of architectural styles, with Gothic vaults, Romanesque arches and a golden coral Renaissance facade. It has 14 chapels, and these contain the remains of many of the country's most famous sons and daughters. The statue of Bishop Bastida bears testimony to a raid by Sir Francis Drake on Santo Domingo in 1586. The two massive doors each weigh two tons.

The cathedral is also the subject of a long running mystery concerning Columbus. When Columbus died in Spain, his body was buried in the cathedral at Seville. Members of his family petitioned for his remains to be exhumed and reburied in Santo Domingo, because of his and their strong associations with the country.

In 1544 his remains were re-buried in the cathedral in Santo Domingo but at the end of the 18th century when Haitian forces occupied the country, his body was removed to Havana Cathedral where it lay for the next 100 years.

Then, in 1898 it was moved again and the mystery deepened: recently, the cathedrals of both Seville and Santa Domingo have claimed to have

Exploits of Francis Drake

In 1585 when war broke out between Britain and Spain, Queen Elizabeth I put Sir Francis Drake in charge of a fleet of 25 fighting ships and dispatched him to the Caribbean to wreak havoc on the Spanish fleet and colonies. He captured Santiago in the Cape Verde Islands, and plundered Cartagena in Columbia and Saint Augustine in Florida, and then attacked Santo Domingo.

Although the pickings in Santo Domingo were not great, Sir Francis Drake established temporary headquarters inside the thick walls of the cathedral while demanding a ransom of 25,000 ducats – the price for his quitting the city. According to legend, Drake struck off the nose and hand of the Bishop's statue with his sword because he was angry at the time taken to deliver the ransom. His rampaging through the Caribbean was so effective that it almost bankrupted the Spanish Crown.

Spain's embarrassment was heightened the following year when Drake sailed into Cadiz harbour and destroyed most of the vessels gathered there in preparation for a counter attack. By the following year, Philip II, the Spanish King, had amassed another Armada, but again, thanks to the daring exploits of Drake, second in charge of the British fleet, the Spanish were routed and almost all their vessels sunk in the English Channel.

Above: The first University in the Americas, Santo Domingo
Below: A typical Parador or roadside cafe

his remains. There is even a suggestion that the remains sent to Cuba in the first place were of a man named Columbus, but not those of Christopher Columbus.

Dominicans believe, of course, that the remains of Columbus did lie beneath the massive marble tomb, and many believe that his body has never left the island.

In 1877 Padre Francisco Billini discovered a small crypt under the cathedral which contained some ashes. These, he declared, were the remains of the explorer. The ashes now lie buried in the magnificent Columbus Lighthouse monument.

The cathedral has many other interesting things to see including a wealth of statues, stonework, old tombs and relics. The cathedral is open from Monday to Saturday between 9am and 6pm. Admission is free and suitable clothing is required.

South of the Cathedral is the Priest's Square and Alley, formerly the cemetery.

Towards the sea

Across Avendia Isabela La Catolica is **Colegia Santa Clara** which dates from 1552 and was a convent of the Clarissa Sisters, members of the Franciscan Order.

Further east the route crosses **Calle de Las Damas** (The Ladies Street), with its cobblestones, quaint archways and old lanterns, so named because it was where the elegant ladies of the court would promenade to catch the early evening breezes rolling in from the sea. The street is believed to be the oldest in the new world, and many of the buildings are more than 500 years old.

Cross over again to **Casa de Bastidas** with its quiet inner courtyard and stunning ceramics. It was the home of Rodrigo de Bastidas who was mayor of the city in 1512.

Fortaleza Ozama

Standing guard by the river mouth at the end of Calle de Las Damas is Fortaleza Ozama, the city's main fortress. The fortress is open daily from 9am to 6pm, except Monday.

The **Torre del Homenaje** (Tower of Homage) stands at the centre of the fort with its massive four feet (1.2m) thick stone walls. It dates from 1502, took five years to finish and was originally the city's main watchtower with sentries on duty on top, and prisoners languishing in cells below. For centuries the tower was used as a prison, especially for condemned men.

There is a huge statue on the esplanade of Gonzalo Fernández de Oviedo, who wrote the chronicle, *"The General History of the Indies"*.

Culture

Cross over Calle de Las Damas into Avenida Padre Billini, turn left into Avenida Isabela La Catolica for the **Oficina de Correos** (Post Office), then turn into Avenida Arzobispo Portes for **Casa de Teatro** (Theatre) ☎ 689-3430) on your right and the **Instituto Dominicana de Cultura Hispanica**.

Churches and hospitals

Then head for the waterfront and the **Monumento Fray Anton de Montesinos**. Turning back inland on Avenida Hostos is the **Convento de los Dominicos** which dates from 1510. In 1538 it was established as the city's university, the first university in the New World.

Take a left turn into Avenida Padre Billini for **Iglesia Regina**, then turn right into Avenida Santome for the **Hospital Padre Bellini** and **Iglesia del Carmen**.

Continue north across El Conde to Avenida Las Mercedes, and turn right for **Iglesia de las Mercedes** built in stone in 1555. Continue east towards the river, turning left into Avenida 19 de Marzo for the **Casa de Tostado**, once the Archbishop's Palace, which houses the **Museum of the Dominican Family** with displays featuring family life in the 19th century. Of interest is the gothic double window, the only one known to be in existence. It is open from Monday to Saturday between 9am and 5pm (☎ 682-4202).

Then head south on Avenida 19 de Marzo for Avenida Luperon.

The ruins of the **Hospital Iglesia di San Nicolas de Bari**, the first hospital ever built in the New World and dating from 1510, are on the corner of Luperon and Avenida Arzobispo Meriuo. Return to El Conde to enjoy the stroll back to Parque Independencia and indulge in a little shopping, wining or dining along the way.

The rest of Santo Domingo

Modern Santo Domingo sprawls north and west of Parque Independencia. The city runs for more than five miles (8km) to the west as far as the golf course and country club, and is bordered in the north by the River Isabela.

Faro a Colon

Faro a Colon (Columbus Lighthouse) is a must. The towering Columbus Lighthouse lies to the east of the River Ozama. The huge complex, built in the shape of a pyramid cross, was opened to the public on 16 October 1992, as part of the country's 500th anniversary celebrations. It is already the country's second leading tourist attraction, after the Cathedral of Santo Domingo.

The complex contains the new lighthouse, as well as several museums and libraries commemorating the voyages and exploits of the explorer. Most important, in the heart of the monument there is a chapel which contains the mortal remains of the great admiral. Next to the chapel, on two levels, are exhibits which have been donated by many nations, as well as a number of museums each focusing on a particular aspect of Columbus's life, his voyages of discovery, the concept and building of the Lighthouse, the Americas and so on.

The monument's most unique feature is the lighting system, which is composed of 151 enormous searchlights and a beam which radiates out for more than 40 miles (64km). When illuminated, the lights project a huge cross into the sky above the site. The idea of the lighthouse was first suggested by Dominican writer and historian Antonio Del Monte y Trejada in 1852 when he wrote, "the glory of the discovery belongs to Columbus... let us erect a statue that will testify to his memory in the most visible and magnificent place in America."

In 1923 at the Fifth International American Conference in Santiago, Chile, it was recommended that the memory of Columbus be honoured by the construction of a lighthouse in Santo Domingo, "with the cooperation of the governments and the peoples of the Americas and with all the nations of the world."

An international competition was staged to come up with plans, and in 1929 student architect J. Gleave submitted the winning plan in the design contest. Trujillo ordered the complex built, but the project ran into difficulties, and it was not until 1987 that Balaguer resumed work.

The lighthouse was officially inaugurated on 6 October, 1992, the day the remains of Columbus were transferred from the cathedral to the chapel. It was opened to the public 10 days later, and that same month, Pope John Paul II, on his third visit to the Dominican Republic, celebrated an open mass. The monument is 7,403 feet (2,257m) long (greater than the Washington Monument), and 1,410 feet (430m) wide, with sloping sides from 604 feet (184m) at the foot to 1,174 feet (358m) at the head. The monument is open from 11am to 5pm daily except Monday, and there is a small admission charge.

The Guácara Taina

The Guácara Taina is another of the city's great attractions. It is a multi-level cultural centre set in a huge cave, featuring folk dancing and music by day, and transforming at night into one of the city's hottest nightspots.

The Jardin Botanico Naçional

The Jardin Botanico Naçional lies between Avenida de los Proceres and Avenida Carlos Perez Ricart to the north. Covering 494 acres (198 hectares), it is one of the largest in the world. There are more gardens to the south, between Avenida de los Proceres and Avenida John F Kennedy.

The main garden has several

Below: *The first oven in the Americas, Santo Domingo*

important collections, including more than 200 different species of palm. There is an orchid pavilion which displays many of the species that can be found in the country, some of which are both tiny and rare and easily overlooked while on the trail. There is also an exquisite Japanese garden.

The gardens are open daily from 9am to 5pm, and there is a small admission charge (☎ 567-6211).

The Malecón

The central part of the city has major thoroughfares, wide tree-lined avenues and the palm fringed Malecón, which runs for several miles along the waterfront. The Malecon, officially called Avenida George Washington, is where the people take their evening stroll, to the inevitable accompaniment of transistor radios, car radios and cassettes. It is the place to gather to watch the Carnival parades go past, or listen to the music during the merengue festival. It is the longest seaside boulevard in the Caribbean and runs for 25 miles (40km).

Mirador Park

Mirador Park and **Paseo de los Indios** run for 5 miles (8km) from the Embajador Hotel to the industrial area of Herera. The park is popular with joggers and walkers, including President Balaguer who walks there every day, during which time the area is closed to traffic. The park is noted for its statues, wall paintings and caves, including Guacara Taina with its subterranean nightclub, one of the city's most popular restaurants.

Mercado Modela

Mercado Modela is one of the main markets with lots of arts and crafts. It is just north of the Colonial City on Avenida Mella, which is also a busy shopping centre. The market, however, is something else. It is noisy, colourful and fun, and a good place to try out one's bargaining skills. It offers a wide range of produce and goods, from locally grown fruits, vegetables, herbs and spices to arts and crafts and the inevitable T-shirts.

Plaza de la Cultura

Plaza de la Cultura is south of Plaza Criolla and just off Avenido Maximo Gomez. It gets its name because it is home to several fine museums including the Modern Art Museum, Museum of Dominican Man, National Library, National Museum of History and Geography and the National Theatre.

The **Museum of the Dominican Man** traces the human settlement of the country from the earliest Amerindians, through pre-Columbian times and the struggle for independence, to the recent past. One exhibit portrays the life of a sugar cane cutter, one of the hardest jobs imaginable. It is open from Tuesday to Saturday between 10am and 5pm (☎ 687-3622).

The **Museo Naçional de Historia y Geographica** is open from Monday to Saturday between 9.30am and 5pm (☎ 686-6668).

The **Museum of Natural History** gives a fascinating insight into Dominicana's natural environment plus exhibits on geology, zoology and space exploration. It is open Tuesday to Sunday from 10.30am to 5.30pm (☎ 689-0106).

Other places of interest

The **Museum of Pre-Hispanic Art**, Avenida San Martin, open Monday to Saturday from 8am to noon. No admission charge (☎ 540-7777).

The **Museum of Trujillo**, Plaza Criolla, a private museum which displays the personal belongings and effects of Trujillo. No admission charge.

The **National Aquarium** opened in the Scientific Park in 1990, and has fresh and salt water exhibits which show the fish in their natural surroundings.

The **Numismatic and Philatelic Museum**, Central Bank, is open Monday to Friday from 8.30am to 3.30pm (☎ 688-6512).

The **Bibliotheca Naçional** is the National Library. It is open between 8am and 5pm Monday to Friday (☎ 686-7872).

The **Palacio Naçional** is on Calle Dr Delgado, and the home of the Congress. Although the marble building looks as if it is as old as some of those in the Colonial City, it was actually built in the 1940's and the Congress moved from their former home in the Palacio de Borgella in 1947. Admission is free but by pre-booked guided tour only.

The **Parque de los Tres Ojos** (Park of Three Eyes) lies north west of Faro a Colon across the Parque Mirador del Este, and is an area of limestone caves and sink holes. There are stalagmites and stalactites surrounding the three underground lagoons in the 50 foot (15m) deep cave surrounded by lush vegetation. From here you can drive along the Avenida de las Americas, so named because on either side are the flags of every nation in the Americas. It is open daily between 8am and 5pm.

The **Parque Zoologico** is about one mile (1.6km) north west of the botanic gardens bordered in the north by the River Isabela. It covers 400 acres (160 hectares) and has almost 5 miles (8km) of roads. It is a cross between zoo, ornamental gardens and pleasure park. It is open daily from 9.30am to 5.30pm and there is a small admission charge.

Theatres

The new open air **Teatro Agua y Luz** (Theatre of Water and Light) features one of the world's largest performing waterfalls. The waterfall was the star attraction at the 1956 World Fair in Santo Domingo, and it has been faithfully reconstructed as the highlight of the theatre which features leading popular music performers. It also has a restaurant and casino.

Teatro Naçional is the home of the National Theatre and the National Symphony Orchestra. The main auditorium seats 1,700 and the acoustics are superb (☎ 687-3191).

Theatre of Fine Arts at Maximo Gomez and Avenida Independencia (☎ 687-2494).

Opposite Page: The Square in La Vega
Above: The streets of Santiago
Below: Santo Domingo Skyline

Eating out in Santo Domingo

$$-$$$ Alcazar,
Hotel Santo Domingo,
local and international
(☎ 221-1511).

$$-$$$ Antoine's,
Sheraton Santo Domingo,
local and international
(☎ 221-6666).

$$ Bachata Rosa Café Concierto,
Creole and international
cuisine to the accompaniment
of live music and dancing
(☎ 688-0969).

$$ Boncherie,
Plaza Merengue,
local and continental
(☎ 472-1603).

$$ Bronco Steak House,
Hotel Cervantes, seafood,
steaks and international
(☎ 686-8161).

$$ Bucanero,
Sans Souci Tourist Harbour,
local, seafood and
international
(☎ 592-2202).

$$-$$$ Cantábrico,
Excellent seafood and international menu, restaurant
bedecked by paintings by
Alberto Ulloa
(☎ 687-5101).

$$ Capri Club,
Padre Billini, Dominicano and
international
(☎ 682-1500).

$$ Captain Crusty,
Avenida Tiradentes, seafood
and Dominican. No telephone.

$$ Che Bandoneon,
Argentinian and French.

$$ Don Pedro,
Avenida Julio Verne, local,
seafood and international
(☎ 688-5737).

$$-$$$ Don Pepe,
Calle Santiago, Spanish and
Dominican. Good seafood and
an impressive wine list
(☎ 689-7612).

$-$$ El Conuco,
Calle Casimro de Moya 152,
Dominican traditional cuisine
in a mock rustic setting. Try
the tripe dishes
(☎ 686-0129).

$$-$$$ El Meson de Castile,
Calle Dr Baez, Spanish and
international. Elegant dining
and noted for its paellas
(☎ 688-4319).

$-$$ Exquesito Café Restaurant French and
deli menu
(☎ 563-6921).

$$ Figaro,
Jaragua Renaissance, Italian
(☎ 221-2222).

$$ **Fonda de la Atarazana**, seafood and creole. Dine in or outside (☎ 689-2900).

$-$$ **Jai Alai**, Spanish and Peruvian, a great dining experience (☎ 688-8389).

$$ **La Mesquita**, Avenida Independencia, Spanish (☎ 687-7090).

$$ **Mario**, Avenida 27 de Febrero, Oriental (☎ 562-4441).

$-$$ **Meson Bari**, Calle Salome Uresa, Creole. Arty and lively.

$$ **Mesón de Castilla**, Spanish and international cuisine (☎ 688-4319).

$$-$$$ **Mesón de la Cava**, International dining and live music in a natural cavern 50 feet below ground (☎ 533-2818).

$$-$$$ **Museo del Jamon**, Las Atarazanas, Spanish (☎ 688-9644).

Ojas, Calle Gazcue, vegetarian (☎ 682-3940).

]$$ **Paco's Bananas**, Calle Danae, Spanish and Creole, very lively and good seafood (☎ 682-3535).

$$ **Palacio de Jade**, Avenido José Herdeia, Oriental (☎ 686-3226).

$$-$$$ **Reina de Espasa**, Spanish and international cuisine and local specialities (☎ 685-2588).

]$$ **Salon de Te**, Las Atarazanas, Middle Eastern (☎ 688-1658).

$$-$$$ **Vesuvio**, on the Malecón, Italian, Spanish and Dominican. One of the best restaurants on the island and usually very busy at all times. You can dine inside or under the stars (☎ 221-3333). If full, try Vesuvio II on the Avenida Tiradentes (☎ 562-6060).

Nightlife

There are hundreds of bars to choose from, especially along El Conde and around the Atarazana. Almost all are lively and noisy.

The liveliest include:

Atlantic Cafe (☎ 565-1841)

Barrauno (☎ 547-2527)

Bella Blue (☎ 689-2911)

Guacara Taina (☎ 530-2666)

Le Petit Chateau (☎ 537-7262)

85

4 EXPLORING & TOURING THE ISLAND

The Dominican Republic has such diverse and exceptional natural beauty that it is well worth making the effort to see a little more of the life and scenery of the island.

In this section, we cover some of the best and most exciting places to visit in the form of self-drive excursions, from which the visitor can select or omit various stages according to personal preference; many of the locations mentioned, however, are also accessible by public transport or included in guided tours.

The island covers quite a large area, and although most places are easily reached within a day's travel, it is sometimes fun to break the trip with an overnight stay in a different location. If planning to travel round the island like this, it is a good idea to arrange accommodation before leaving. Most hotels will ring round to make suitable reservations.

Santo Domingo is the focal point of many tours and services in the south, and is therefore a convenient base from which to begin trips along the south coast both to the west, towards Pedernales, and to the east, towards Punta Cana, and also into the Central Mountains to the north.

If you are based at a resort in the south, the north coast is a fair distance – Puerto Plata is some 127 miles (205 km) from Santo Domingo – but it is still well worth taking the opportunity to visit the northern part of the country, especially the spectacular north coastline.

Santiago makes a good central touring base in the north, with the added advantage of accommodation being usually available here if coastal hotels are full.

Getting around

Getting round the Dominican Republic is part of the fun of visiting the country. The best way to see the island is by hire car so that you can take your own time and detour off the main route whenever the fancy takes you (see car hire section). There are, however, many tours

Opposite: Playa Dorada

available. There are also small planes for charter for those who can afford them and wish to get to their destination quickly; aerial views of the island are truly stunning.

By road

There are more than 12,400 miles (20,000km) of highways and secondary roads throughout the country, linking all main towns and cities. All areas are accessible by hire car, taxi, bus or ground tour operator.

The main road runs from Santo Domingo on the south coast, through Santiago to Monte Cristi on the north west coast. It is usually very busy, and the road surface is often in need of repair because of damage caused by the volume of traffic. However, there are major road works underway to widen the road to dual carriageway along most of its length.

The roads along the north and south east coasts and through the eastern part of the country are very good. There are fewer roads in the south west, and travel into the central highlands is an adventure in itself.

By rail

Train travel is not an option. There is only one Government-owned railway running through the Cibao Valley between La Vega and the port of Sanchez on Bahia de Samaná which only carries freight. All other freight is transported round the country by trucks and lorries. Other railway lines that you see are only used to carry sugar cane and workers between the fields and the sugar mills.

Guaguas

Guaguas are generally crowded, always noisy with speakers blaring out at full volume, and the drivers often travel as fast as possible because the more trips they make, the more they earn. Always drive with care if following mini-buses, although this will not happen often as they will overtake you at the first opportunity and zoom off into the distance. They do have a habit of suddenly screeching to a halt to pick up or drop off a passenger, so be careful. Having said that, however, do not be discouraged. These mini-buses are a great way to get around, and an entertainment in themselves.

By bus

Buses (guaguas) and private mini-buses / taxis (carros publicos) operate within the main towns and cities and out to the immediate surrounding districts. Yellow public buses are cheapest but they do not seem to operate to any schedule and it is a question of waiting until one comes along – and when it does, it is usually crowded.

Mini-buses/taxis operate along fixed routes. These are either Japanese mini-vans or large cars which cost a little more, but are much quicker. They operate throughout the day, usually from dawn to dusk, taking workers and shoppers into town and then taking them back again.

In the countryside, you can just flag a bus down if you want to catch it, while in towns they usually leave from the main square either when they are full, or when there are enough passengers on board to make it worthwhile.

In Santo Domingo, many of the mini-buses leave from around Parque Enriquillo, just north of the Colonial City. Always make sure the bus is heading in your direction, or you could get stranded in the countryside by the time you discover it is not. In rural areas, guaguas are often open pick up trucks.

By coach

There is an extensive coach network which runs between the main towns and cities, with most services operating out of Santo Domingo. This means that if you are staying on the east coast and want to get to the north coast, you may have to travel in to Santo Domingo to catch your connection, and this may involve an overnight stay.

The north coast is well serviced, however, with several coaches a day travelling to and from Santo Domingo. Tickets can be reserved in advance but that does not always guarantee a seat, and the golden rule is to get there early. If you have a ticket but get there late, someone else may be sold a ticket for your seat.

Coach services operate from various terminals in Santo Domingo, and usually from the main squares in smaller towns. There are several companies operating the coach services. These include Terrabus (☎541-2080), which operate from their Plaza Criolla Terminus in Santo Domingo.

The coaches are usually in good condition, provide loud, action-packed videos en route and often have snacks and drinks for sale. Caribe Tours operate from their terminal at the corner of Avenidas Leopoldo Navarro and 27 de Febrero (☎687-3171), and Calle 12 de Julio in Puerto Plata, and Avenida Estrella Sadhala in Santiago.

Metro Buses (☎566-6587) run from the corner of Avenidas Winston Churchill and Hatuey in Santo Domingo, Mota Saad (☎688-7775) operate from Avenida Independencia, and Apolo Taxi (☎541-9595) also operates from Santo Domingo.

By taxi

Taxis are widely available at the airport, outside hotels, and in the major towns and cities, but these are not metered and you should always agree a price for the trip before you set off. Also agree the currency in which you are dealing.

By air

There are international airports at Punta Caucedo, 15 miles (24km) east of Santo Domingo, and at Puerto Plata on the north coast. The airport at Santiago is also capable of taking small jets and larger propeller aircraft. There are also several small airfields around the country open to small charter aircraft. These include Herrera Airport on the western outskirts of Santo Domingo. Bávaro Sunflight is a new local airline that operates between Santo Domingo and the main tourist areas.

Tour 1: The South West and Lake Enriquillo

Distance for the trip is about 500 miles, but this is reduced to 350 miles if Barahona and Pedernales in the far south west are not taken in. The main roads are good thoughout this tour.

Take Carretera Sanchez west out of Santo Domingo and join Highway 2 signposted to Bajos de Haina.

San Cristobal Province

The city of San Cristobal was founded on the banks of the River Nigua, close to the fortress built on the orders of Columbus, and it has grown rapidly in recent years with thousands of small shacks clinging to the surrounding hillsides.

The city has a number of fine buildings, however, most of them a legacy of Trujillo who was born in the town, and retained a great affection for it even though he lived most of his life in the splendour of his palace in Santo Domingo. He was responsible for the central plaza and the church, and there is even the mausoleum he had built for himself, although his remains were taken to France. He was born in **Casa las Coabas**, which overlooks the town and is now run down. Because of his record, it has not been high on the list of places to be restored, but it is open to the public between 9am and 5pm. Also overlooking the town is **Castillo del Cerro**, another of Trujillo's palaces. It was in San Cristóbal that the country's first Constitution was signed on 6 November, 1844.

Of interest are the **Caves at El Pomier**, Trujillo's unused **Mahogany House**, the **Baths of La Toma** and the **Church and Caves of Santa Maria**, where the patron saint's feast day is celebrated with singing, drumming and lively dancing.

There are good beaches at **Najaya** and **Nigua**. At **Punta Palenque** there is a 1.25mile (2km) long horseshoe-shaped beach.

Bani

Further along Highway 2 is Bani, at the heart of an important sugar cane and coffee producing area, and the birthplace of Independence hero Maximo Gomez on 18 November, 1836. There is a town museum, a Church – Our Lady of Regla, and nearby is the white sand beach of Los Almendros, which is developing as a tourist resort. The town is named after Bani, one of Caonabo's most trusted lieutenants. The word also means 'land of plentiful water', in the Taino language.

Above: Sosúa beach   ***Below***: Barahona Bay on the road to Paraiso

At **Puerto Hermoso** there are huge salt deposits, and Caldera Bay is the home of one of the country's main naval bases at Las Calderas.

Peravia

The Peravia region is noted for its goats, and at **Paya** you can get delicious goat milk candy. The area has a lot of wild oregano which the goats graze on, and it is this that gives the goats of this region a very special flavour. All along this route you will find roadside stalls offering fruit from oranges to green coconuts, which provide a wonderfully refreshing drink.

Ocoa Bay

Corbanito is on the eastern side of Ocoa Bay and is along a spectacular stretch of beach which runs for 6 miles (10km), although the colour of the sand varies from white at Corbanito where there is safe swimming because of the inshore reef, to grey at Palmar de Ocoa, where the beach shelves steeply and offers good fishing. At **Monte Rio**, at the head of the bay there is another lovely beach.

Azua

Continue round the coast past Bahia de Ocoa to Azua. It was founded in 1504 by Diego Velázquez, conqueror of Cuba, who called it Azua de Compostela. It was granted a coat of arms by the King of Spain in 1508 and has been sacked at least three times by French pirates who burned it to the ground. Jean Jacques Dessalines, who declared Haiti independent on 1 January 1804, also ordered the town destroyed after invading the country in 1805. In 1844 and 1849, the Haitians razed it again. Not far from the town are the remains of the old colonial city of **Pueblo Viejo**. Azua is also noted for its succulent melons.

Into the mountains

Continue about 10 miles (16km) until the road splits. Keep right on Highway 2 and then take the secondary road on your right leading into the mountains and **Padre Las Casas** and **Bohechio**. Then return to the main road and turn right heading west for San Juan. There is another mountain road north to Juan de Ferrera, but continue on Highway 2 to Las Matas de Farfan and El Llano just south of the main road, and Comendador close to the Haitian border.

Turn south on Highway 47 for Hondo Valle and **La Descubierta**. Just out of town there are a number of Arawak petroglyphs (stone carvings) on the cliff.

Lake Enriquillo

Close by is Lago Enriquillo which is the largest salt water lake in the Caribbean, almost 23 miles (37km) long and 11 miles (18km) across at its widest point. It lies 140 feet (43m) below sea level and is the only one in the world inhabited by crocodiles!

Isla Cabritos (Goat Island) in the middle of the lake is 5 miles (8km) long and is a national park. It was used to free-graze goats and is now an important wildlife refuge with two species of iguana and the rare American crocodile. Birdlife includes flamingo, roseate spoonbills and water rails. You must have first obtained permission from the national parks headquarters in Santo Domingo, and then report to the park office in **La Descubierta,** before crossing over to the island by boat.

It is possible to make a circular tour all round the lake on Highway 48, through Postrer Rio, Villa Jaragua, Neiba, Duverge and back to Jimani. Our route passes the southern shore of the lake to Neiba and then continues on Highway 48 past Tamayo to the junction with Highway 44.

At this point you can either continue east on Highway 44 to Azua for Highway 2 which runs back into Santo Domingo, or you can head south and explore the desert like landscape of Pedernales.

The Pedernales region

Travelling south on Highway 44, turn off right to visit Cabral or continue south past Corbanito, a 6 mile (9km) stretch of beaches, including Bahia de Corbanito, Palmar de Ocoa, Playa Chiquita and Monte Rio, to the small, industrial town of **Barahona** with its very lively central square.

The town was founded in 1802 by the French General Toussaint l'Ouverture. It was formerly ruled by the legendary female chieftain Anacona, and was also the home of the internationally acclaimed folk singer Casandra Damirón. The province is noted for its large salt, gypsum and bauxite deposits, and in 1927 the port of Barahona saw the first cargo and passenger service plying between the Dominican Republic, Port Au Prince, the U.S., Virgin Islands and Cuba.

The peninsula boasts many fine beaches such as La Saladilla, Rio Caso, El Quemaito, Bahoruco, La Ciénaga, El Desfiladero de los Amargados, San Rafael, Los Patos and Paraiso, but inland, this south west corner of the country is remote and desolate, The vegetation, is impressive however, especially if you like cactus. There are giant organ pipe cactus and prickly pear. The secluded sandy beaches have no facilities, however, so it is wise to take a picnic and plenty of liquids.

Follow the coast road through Paraiso and Baoruco, where there is a small beach and hotel. **Enriquillo** is only a small fishing village but with lovely beaches.

Oviedo is a small fishing village with safe, sandy beaches. The road then cuts across to **Pedernales** in the extreme south west, on the coastal border with Haiti. There may well be some military activity anywhere close to the Haitian border, and it is not unusual to be flagged down and have your vehicle searched. It was in the nearby Naoruco Mountains that Taino chief Enriquillo waged his guerrilla war against the Spanish in the 1520s.

Jaragua National Park

Although Villa Jaragua lies on the northern shores of Lake Enriquillo, the Jaragua National Park covers 500 square miles (1300 sq.km) of the south western tip of the country, a desert area of cacti and bleak, limestone coastline.

The park includes the island of Beata just offshore and west of Cabo Beata, and both the mainland and island are important birdlife sanctuaries. Beata is said to have been a refuge of the pirate Cofresi. His treasure is rumoured to be buried in the area around **Punta Iglesia**, and on the beach near the village of Juan Esteban, a casket filled with jewels was found.

This section of the trip is well worthwhile, but you have to return along the same route, and then continue to Azua and the final leg back to Santo Domingo.

Eating Out

There are some bars and paradors offering traditional dishes and drinks, as well as roadside stalls selling fruit and snacks. If you are planning to spend the day on the beach you need to take your own food and drink.

Tour 2: The South East and Punta Cana

This south eastern part of the country is one of the richest agricultural belts in the Caribbean and fast becoming one of the main tourist areas as well. The coastal plain stretches for more than 110 miles (177km) and is up to 28 miles (45km) wide. There are vast sugar cane estates, about 10 sugar mills and huge cattle ranches.

Above: Casa Bonita, Barahona **Below:** Waterfall and pools at St. Rafael

Take Avenida de las Americas out of Santo Domingo which joins Highway 3. The road follows the coastline to **La Caleta,** where there is a Park and Museum with an exhibit of an Arawak village and burial ground. La Caleta is a fishing village set in a large cove, and it is a favourite spot for artists because of the views and spectacular sunsets.

Boca Chica

Continue past the international airport to the tourist resort of Boca Chica, 15 miles (24km) from the capital. It was originally a small fishing village and it became a popular week-end retreat for the people of Santo Domingo. Today, this is one of the island's most popular beach areas and at weekends and public holidays, it is packed with locals. Whilst the beach is busy, the atmosphere is extraordinary, and the music deafening as each group seems to have its own radio or cassette player, most turned to full volume and a different station!

There is a large choice of accommodation along the waterfront from resorts and large hotels to small inns. The larger resort hotels include the Don Juan Beach Resort, Boca Chica Resort, and the new 458 room Hamaca Beach Hotel and Casino, which has grown luxuriously on the site formerly occupied by a small 22 room hotel. The town, which offers a wide range of bars and restaurants and many different cuisines, hosts the annual international blue marlin fishing competition.

San Pedro del Macoris region

Juan Dolio is another lovely beach area although not as crowded as Boca Chica, and the sands are fringed with palm trees and laid-back bars where you can enjoy a drink and watch the world drift past. There are a number of small hotels and larger all-inclusive complexes, such as the 313 room Diamond Costa Caribe right on the beach. The same company also operates the Caribbean Village Trops, Caribbean Village Costa Linda and the Caribbean Village Decameron Club with its popular casino.

Many international hotel groups have decided this is where they need to be and have opened or are building, resort hotels in the area: these include Occidental Hotels and the Sheraton group. The 283 room Capella Beach Renaissance was opened in 1994. One of the island's best restaurants is L'Ecrivesse, in the 260 room

Talanquera Country and Beach Resort. It features Caribbean haute cuisine and has deservedly won a number of international awards both for its food and its exceptional wine list.

There are coral reefs offshore, and the beach at the Embassy Beach Resort is protected by a natural sea wall consisting of two sections of reef which can be reached by strong swimmers. There are several other hotels in the area. This stretch of coastline has many fine beaches such as Caribe Beach, a large coconut palm-fringed cove popular with surfers, Guayacanes and Villas Del Mar.

San Pedro de Macoris town

Continue to the town of San Pedro de Macoris which was founded at the beginning of the 19th century by European and Middle Eastern immigrants. It became a province in 1882 and was the home of the country's first telephone exchange. In 1884 the first telephone call between San Pedro and Santo Domingo was made when President Ulises Heureaux-Lilis spoke to General Francisco Gregorio Billini. Pan American Airways used to land its passenger seaplanes in the estuary of the nearby Higuamo River.

The town's prosperity was built on sugar cane, and it was so affluent that it used to be known as the Sultan of the East. The wealth is reflected in the many fine old homes with neoclassical and Victorian architecture, while the smaller homes of migrant workers reflect housing styles found in the Windward and Leeward Islands.

These workers introduced the Momise, a dance based on the English Mummers drama. It is a highly ritualised dance form, which can also be quite erotic and sensuous. It is one of the highlights of the town's feast day on 29th June.

The town is also the home of the Universidad Central del Este (UCE), and the Tetelo Vargas baseball stadium. Of interest is the neoclassical Church of Saint Peter on the banks of the river, with its tower which acts as a town landmark. The town's bus station is in front of the church, with services to Santo Domingo and other locations further east.

La Romana Region

La Romana town was founded by Juan Esquivel in 1502, and is the main town of the region, which is an important sugar cane and livestock rearing area. Visitors come here, however, for the fabulous palm-fringed beaches and up-market resorts in La Romana and **Punta Cana** on the eastern tip of the island, with its own international airport.

The coast between Bávaro, Macao, Arena Garda, Cortecito, Cabeza de Toro and Punta Cana is one of the most beautiful stretches of beach in the Caribbean – 20 miles (32km) of pure white sand and more than 300,000 coconut palms. The resorts are discretely sited a little way from the beach so as not to interfere with the view.

Casa de Campo

Casa de Campo in La Romana, has been described as the ultimate resort for sports enthusiasts. An indication of how upmarket it is, there being four polo fields available for experienced riders. It boasts three championship golf courses, including the famous 'Teeth of the Dog' course designed by Pete Dye, 13 clay tennis courts, 20 swimming pools, a stable of more than 550 horses, and ponies for polo or trail riding; there is a private 245 acre (86 hectare) shooting centre featuring the world's tallest sporting clays tower and run by Michael Rose, one of England's leading instructors, squash, racquetball, fitness centres, a private marina and watersports. The resort covers 7,000 acres (2,800 hectares) and was designed by Oscar de la Renta.

The complex also includes **Altos de Chavón**, a delightful "historic" village situated on top of the cliffs, with pretty houses built of coral stone and well-tended gardens bursting with exotic blooms. It is not surprising that the town has attracted a lot of artists because everywhere you look there are scenes to be painted, and the views are spectacular. The centre of the village is a warren of narrow cobbled streets and alleys, radiating from the Iglesia St. Stanislas. The stunning 5,000 seat amphitheatre which affords magnificent views, has played host to stars such as Frank Sinatra and Julio Iglesias.

The Archaeology Museum has regional exhibits and an excellent pre-Hispanic collection (☎ 688-3139). There are also several restaurants, bars and art galleries. It is difficult to persuade some people that the town is not really centuries, let alone decades old. The town was created on an architect's drawing board in the 1970s, and superbly designed down to the finest Gothic detail. There are tours to Altos de Chavón from Casa de Campo and many other resorts.

This stretch of coastline is fast becoming one of the hottest tourist destinations around, and the beaches at Macao,

Above: Casa de Campo beach ***Below****: La Romana beach road*

Arena Gorda, Cortecito, Bávaro, Cabeza de Toro and Punta Cana are rated in the world's top 25.

Catalina Island

Just offshore is the uninhabited Isla Catalina which has fabulous beaches, and passage across is usually possible from Casa de Campo where there are lots of boats. There are no facilities on the island so take a picnic and plenty of soft drinks.

The island lies in phosphorescent **Catalina Bay**. The bay is seen to best effect on a moonless night when the special luminescent plankton cast their beautiful blue glow across the sea. You can take a boat ride into the bay and the movement of the boat or your hand in the water, causes the plankton to move in sparkling light patterns around you.

Other beaches

Playa Minitas is a man-made beach with limited access because it is at the end of private land, but it offers a wide range of watersports; the **Bayahibe** Beach is even more secluded. Close by is the 470 room Club Dominicus Beach resort hotel. The road is bumpy and difficult after rain, but the journey is worth the effort. Cross by boat from Bayahibe to Saona, where there are a number of beach restaurants.

River Yuma region

Highway 3 continues east to connect with Highway 4. At the junction, the right turn leads to the small town of **San Rafael del Yuma** on the river. The most interesting site is the former fortified home of Ponce de Leon who lived there from 1505 to 1508 before sailing for Puerto Rico and on to Florida. Further along the road, is the small fishing village of **Boca de Yuma** at the mouth of the river.

Parque Nacional del Este

Much of the land to the south west of Boca de Yuma, including the island of **Saona** off the end of the peninsula, lies within the Parque Naçional del Este, the national park of the east. The western entrance is at Bayahibe, close to La Romana. There are many trails through the park but you are advised to hire a guide. The park contains forest, mangrove swamp and coastal habitats and is the home of the manatee. Dolphins can sometimes be seen offshore, and among the many bird species is the small endemic crown pigeon.

Saona is the largest of the offshore islands and covers 80 square miles (208 sq.km). It has a population of about 1,500 and fishing is the main occupation although some people hunt pigeons and wild pigs.

Higuey

Heading inland to the north, Highway 4 runs through the heart of sugar-cane and cattle country. Higuey is an historic market town founded in 1494 and built round the Basilica de Nuestra Sesora de la Merced. The church is said to have been built on the site of a battle in which Spanish settlers fought off a Carib attack, and because of this it has been a place of pilgrimage for hundreds of years, especially on 21 January and 16 August.

In the 1950s, the towering Basilica de Nuestra Sesora de Altagracia was built to accommodate the growing number of pilgrims and tourists. The new church is built to represent a giant pair of hands held together in prayer.

Off the main route, this is farming country and paved roads give way to dirt tracks, with many of the farmers getting around on horseback.

The South East coastal region

The road east leads to the magnificent beaches around **Punta Cana**.

Once covered in dense jungle which reached down to the shoreline, there are now stunning resorts set in landscaped gardens and championship golf courses. Not all the forest has been cleared, however, and at the Punta Cana Beach Resort, with 350 rooms and villas, you can walk along paths through the dense woodland to natural springs where swimming is a wonderful experience. The Club Med Punta Resort was the first hotel in the area when it opened in 1981, and now has a new 18 hole championship golf course designed by Robert Trent Jones.

Bavaro

The next major resort area is around Playa Bavaro where there are many large hotels. The Barceló Group alone operates five hotels in the resort with a total of 1,800 rooms, including a casino, an 18-hole golf course, a wide range of sporting facilities and conference rooms. Newly opened hotels include the Bávaro Palace, the Riu Palace Macao Resort, and the Meliá Bávaro Beach Resort which was beautifully designed to harmonise with its natural location. There are still more than 30 miles (50km) of white sand beach along this coastline, and it is only a question of time before more hotels appear.

There are many lovely, secluded beaches along this stretch of coastline as far as Miches, but the Atlantic rollers can kick up a surf so swimmers need to take care. The onshore winds do offer some welcome relief from the sun if you are soaking it up on the beach.

Hato Mayor region

The drive through this area is well worthwhile for those who have the time; the scenery and wildlife is interesting and varied.

Highway 104 continues along the northern coast to **Miches**, and passes through a stretch of sparsely populated farming country to Sabana de la Mar, from where a ferry can be taken across to Samaná. The inland route is through El Seibo and Hato Mayor and then takes Highway 103 north to El Valle and Sabana de la Mar.

For the return journey, retrace the same route to Hato Mayor, and then take Highway 23 west to Monte Plata, continuing north to Sabana Grande de Boya, and on to its junction with Highway 11. Then drive south to Yamasa, and take Highway 13 back to Santo Domingo, taking in the Columbus lighthouse on the outskirts and entering the capital along Avenida Espansa and the Mella Bridge.

Eating out in the south

Boca Chica

$$ **Casa Del Mar**, Avenida Nunez, seafood and steaks (☎ 523-4404)

$$ **Los Corales**, Hotel Hamaca, international (☎ 523-4611).

$$ **Marie Pierre**, Villa Sans Soucy, Canadian (☎ 523-4461).

$$ **Neptune's Club**, seafood (☎ 523-4703).

Higuey

La Mamma Venezia, Punta Cana Beach Resort, local, seafood and international (☎ 688-4032).

Juan Dolio

El Pescador, Metro Hotel, local, seafood and international (☎ 526-1710).

La Romana

$-$$ **Cafe del Sol**, Altos de Chavón, Italian (☎ 523-3333).

$$-$$$ **Casa del Rio**, Altos de Chavón, continental (☎ 523-3333).

$$ **El Patio**, Altos de Chavón, local, Spanish and international (☎ 523-3333).

$$ **El Pescador**, Altos de Chavón, seafood (☎ 523-3333).

$$-$$$ **El Sombrero**, Altos de Chavón, Canadian (☎ 523-3333).

$$-$$$ **Lago Grill**, Casa de Campo, local, seafood and international (☎523-3333).

$-$$ **La Piazzetta**, Altos de Chavón, Italian (☎ 523-3333).

$-$$ **Tropicana**, Casa de Campo, local, seafood and Spanish (☎ 523-3333).

Tour 3: The Central Highlands and Mount Duarte

The fastest route north is on the new Highway 1 (the Duarte Highway), which runs north as far as Santiago and then west to Monte Cristi, close to the border with Haiti.

Below: Playa Dorada

An alternative route is to head west out of Santo Domingo on Highway 2, past the poorer sprawling outer districts of the city, through Bani and then inland on Highway 41 which runs through the Cordillera Central, the country's highest mountains and location of some of its most spectacular scenery.

Costanza

Constanza is a charming hill town set in the mountains and surrounded by sweet smelling pine forests and spectacular views. Many wealthy Dominicans have built homes in and around Constanza, which escapes the summer heat of the coast because of its altitude. The Constanza Valley is the highest in the country, but the special micro-climate means winter temperatures are several degrees higher than in surrounding areas, and allow the cultivation of potatoes, vegetables, strawberries, apples and flowers.

South of Constanza are the **Aguas Blancas**, two waterfalls which can be seen from the road and which can be reached on foot. The walk is not easy and involves some scrambling but, if you persevere, a cooling swim in the water at the foot of the falls is a just reward.

From Constanza, Highway 28 continues north through Jarabacoa and rejoins Highway 1 at La Vega.

Pico Duarte expedition

For those who enjoy backpacking, this is a rare mountain treat, but not to be undertaken too lightly: it will take four days to trek in and out, and remember that you will have to carry all your food, warm clothes for the evening, waterproofs and sleeping bag. Wear suitable clothing and stout, non-slip footwear because conditions along the trail can be treacherous, especially after a rain shower.

Jarabacoa is the best place from which to start any expedition into the mountains. There are several paths to the summit, but the most common is through Monabao and **La Cienga**. Always inform the park wardens at La Cienga when you are about to set off, and check in on your return.

A guide is essential, not only because it is easy to get lost in the densely forested mountains and valleys, but because you will miss so much along the way. Something that looks like a leaf, the guide will reveal as a giant moth, and tiny, rare orchids hidden among rocks are easily passed by if not pointed out by an expert.

Pico Duarte is not only the highest peak in the Dominican Republic, but in all the Caribbean islands. The mountain used to be called Pico la Pelona (the Bald Mountain), because of the sparsity of vegetation close to the summit. For a short time, Trujillo re-named it Pico Trujillo, but now the name has been changed again to commemorate the Dominican champion of independence, Juan Pablo Duerte.

A bust of Duarte stands on the summit, for those fit and able enough to make the climb.

Other places of interest

There are two national parks in the central mountains – Bermudez and Ramirez.

The **Jimenoa Waterfall** is south of Jarabacoa, near El Salto, and reached by quite a steep path which leads down to the 100 feet (30m) falls. The walk back up might leave you puffing.

Tour 4: The Amber Coast

The northern coast is nicknamed the Amber Coast because of the large deposits of amber found there. It is where Columbus first stepped ashore more than 500 years ago and where today, tourists flock to take advantage of the golden sands and lively beach resorts.

On a good day, the direct journey from Santo Domingo to Puerto Plata on the north coast, will take between 3 and 4 hours.

The road north

Take Highway 1 out from Santo Domingo through Villa Altagracia and Piedra Blanca, to **Bonao**, which is half way between Santo Domingo and Santiago.

Bonao has expanded rapidly in the last few years as mining interests have moved in to exploit the rich mineral deposits in the surrounding hills, especially bauxite and nickel. Despite the expansion and the new buildings, the centre of the town has retained much of its old world charm.

La Vega

The next main town, La Vega, is in the fertile Cibao Valley and supports thousands of small farms. Families tend their tiny plots of land, raising crops in the rich brown earth, and living in small thatched bohios by the roadside or perched up on the hillsides. The Cibao Valley runs between the Central Mountains and the Cordillera Septentrional, and is the agricultural heart of the country, famous in particular for its quality tobacco.

Santo Cerro

Just north of La Vega is the Santo Cerro, worth ascending for the spectacular views, and its historical significance. It was the place where the first cross was planted in the Americas by Columbus in 1492; it had been presented to him by Queen Isabela of Spain as he set sail from the port of Palos de Moguer. Legend has it that during a battle between the Spanish and the Indians, their chief Guarionex tried to burn the cross but it would not catch alight. A piece of the cross has been preserved.

Nearby are the ruins of **Vega Real**, the original settlement in the valley, which was destroyed by in 1562. The residents of Vega Real moved along the valley and founded La Vega.

Santiago

Santiago, or to give the city its full name, Santiago de los Triento Caballeros, was founded by Columbus's brother Bartholomew in 1495, on the site now occupied by Pueblo Viejo. It is the country's second largest city with a population of about 700,000, and is a marked contrast from Santo Domingo.

Santiago commands a brilliant defensive position on top of a gorge overlooking the river. The city has a much gentler pace of life than either Santo Domingo or the busy tourist areas on the north coast, and is not usually on the tourist map, but it is worth a visit. There are some fine old Colonial town houses built during the last century by rich landowners, at a time when the surrounding agricultural countryside provided much of the country's wealth. The colonial homes are identified by their large windows, wrought iron grills and tiled porticos which contrast with the ornate gingerbread style of the adjoining Victorian buildings.

The **Museo del Tabaco** on Calle 30 de Marzo, shows the fascinating and complicated process of converting tobacco leaves into world-class cigars.

The **Museo de Arte Folklorico** in the city centre, is housed in a charming old building, and features local arts and crafts. Admission is free and the museum is run by the son of the founder who collected most of the exhibits. Santiago is famous for its carnival, and the museum houses many of the elaborate prize winning masks made for this celebration over the years.

The **Cathedral de Santiago Apostol** in Parque Duarte, is a mix of Gothic and neo-Classic architecture built in the 19th century. It has a beautiful mahogany altar.

The City Museum is in a 19th century palace with exhibits from the city's colourful and historic past. The city also boasts a number of rum distilleries which can be visited, and most offer tours and tastings.

At **Jacagua** on the northern outskirts of the city are the ruins of the first colonial town on the site. Above the town stands a 200 foot (61m) tall memorial built by Trujillo as another example of his self-aggrandisement. It has now been re-dedicated to honour the heroes of 1844, when the Dominicans rose up and finally threw out the Haitians who had occupied the country for 22 years. The monument is only spectacular because of its height.

Gurabo, in the mountains to

Tobacco

Most of the tobacco is grown in small fields which are lovingly cultivated by one family. Seeds or seedlings are planted in the rich soil in November, and after three months the plants are up to five feet (1.5m) tall. The harvest can start as early as January but it is usually in March, and the leaves are picked by hand, with the strongest flavoured leaves furthest from the ground. Like grapes, some years produce much better crops than others.

Each leaf is graded individually and then cured according to its intended use. Some leaves are picked for the body they give to the finished cigar, others for aroma, others for an even burn and so on.

The leaves are first cured in the sun where they turn from green to brown: then they are cured in the distinctive casas de tobaco, or drying sheds, for about six weeks. They are then piled in heaps to 'ferment', before being packed in bales and shipped to the sorters, who strip the leaves from their stems, and grade them according to their colour. They are then allowed to ferment again, to lose some of their tar, and then they are aged – anything from one to three years.

They are then taken to the factory where the leaves are sorted again for strength and colour. The leaves for the very finest cigars are taken away for a further period of ageing, while the rest, after more than 80 separate processes, are blended and finally made into cigars. The most skilled workers can produce up to 150 hand-made cigars a day. The cigars are banded, boxed and given a final inspection before being sent out.

the north west of Santiago, is famous for its weavers, who are especially noted for their braided hats.

Using Santiago as a base, there are two tours we would recommend in opposite directions to each other, both rich in a mixture of history, beach, shopping, nightlife and wildlife.

4A: The North West & Puerto Plata

From Santiago head south on Highway 16 to Janico and follow it west to San Jose de la Mantas, Moncion, Sabaneta and Dajabon, close to the Haitian border.

Turn north on Highway 45 towards **Monte Cristi**.

The landscape changes dramatically as you drive towards the coast. The area is in a rain shadow and annual rainfall is often less than 30 inches (76cm) a year. The wind in this north western most part of the country adds to the bleak landscape of cacti, scrub vegetation and shallow salt lagoons.

Monte Cristi

Monte Cristi, which lies at the foot of the promontory El Morro, is said to have been the inspiration for Alexander Dumas' novel the Count of Monte Cristo. El Morro is a Spanish word which has no easy English translation and its meaning ranges from a 'headland' to 'a fantastic shape'. If you look at El Morro from a distance, the two rocks appear to resemble a camel lying down with the its head resting on the ground.

The area boasts more days of sunshine than elsewhere on the island, the sun usually making an appearance on no less than 351 days each year. The waters offshore are strewn with wrecks, and more than 180 galleons are believed to have foundered here.

Manzanilla

To the west of Monte Cristi and close to Pepillo Salcedo and the border with Haiti, is the port of Manzanilla in the bay of the same name. The natural deep water port used to be one of the busiest in the country, but it has declined in recent years although it still receives the banana boats from the U.K. and it is still one of the main ports for the export of bananas. Plans are under discussion to use the deep water anchorage for visiting cruise ships.

The **Parque Naçional El Morro** is to the north east of Monte Cristi, and this undeveloped area of land teems with wildlife, with many species of waders and seabirds.

Offshore is **Cayo Cabrito** – Goat Island, which gets its name because it was common for sailors to leave goats on small islands so that they could breed and provide a supply of fresh meat for future voyages.

History

The coastline is a little desolate to start with because of the low rainfall, but it starts to become greener and by the time you reach **Villa Isabela** the scenery is stunning. Isabela was the site of Columbus's first settlement on the island, although it did not last long. There is little to be seen other than the sites of various archaeological digs, but a small church has been built to commemorate the place where the first christian mass was celebrated, and there is a small museum containing some of the artifacts unearthed nearby.

Columbus landed about 1,000 settlers here in 1493 during his second voyage of discovery, but the site was ill-chosen. The settlers were constantly attacked by the Caribs and many died from disease in what was to them a very unhealthy climate. When Columbus returned, he evacuated the settlers and established the new settlement of Santo Domingo, on the south coast.

Beaches

This is a beautiful stretch of coastline with mile after mile of glorious beaches of dazzling white sand, swaying palms, turquoise seas and offshore reefs. There are several resort developments along the coast, mostly around Puerta Plata and further east, but large stretches of shoreline offer secluded bays and coves, and miles of endless sands which you can often have all to yourself, as at **Punta Rucia**.

The fishing village of **Luperon** also has a fine beach – a wide stretch of sand with palm trees for shade, and a blossoming tourist industry. It has become a popular destination for yachtsmen, scuba divers and anglers. There are bars and restaurants where you can enjoy lunch and a refreshing drink.

Costambar has a lovely beach protected by coral reefs, while almond trees offer shade on the edge of the sand.

Cofresi has another fabulous beach, more than one mile (1.6km) long, and although it is close to Puerto Plata it doesn't seem to attract the crowds like the beaches to the east of the neighbouring resort. There is one hotel where you can get refreshments.

Above left: Santiago Monument ***Above right:*** Santiago Cathedral
Below: Puerto Plata main square

Puerto Plata

Puerto Plata was one of the first settlements on the island, and was founded at the beginning of the 16th century, with the impressive Cordillera Septentrional as a backdrop. The town, which means Silver Harbour, has a very turbulent history. Presumably the lure of silver attracted pirates and the port was repeatedly attacked. Eventually a massive fort, **Fortaleza de San Felipe**, was built on the promontory to the east of the harbour. It is the only 16th century colonial structure left in the town. It was started in 1541 and finished in 1577, but this did not discourage attacks and by the end of the century it had fallen into the hands of the pirates. In 1605, Spanish troops attacked the town, drove the pirates out and then destroyed the buildings to discourage them from returning.

The fort was converted by Trujillo into a prison, and is now a museum documenting the history of the fort and town. It is open daily except Thursday between 9am and 5pm although it closes for a lengthy lunch and siesta break. There is a small admission charge.

In front of the fort is a memorial to General Gregorio Luperon, one of the country's greatest national heroes.

Eventually a new settlement developed around the port, and Puerto Plata is now the main town on the north coast with a thriving tourist industry, although most of the resort development is along the beaches to the east of the town.

The Gregorio Luperón International Airport serves Puerto Plata and the neighbouring resort towns, and has recently been expanded to cope with demand well into the 21st century.

Puerto Plata itself is a typical Caribbean town laid out in a grid, with a central park, and with its painted wooden houses decorated with the ornate fretwork known as "gingerbread", and a wealth of shops and restaurants. Sights to see include **Iglesia San Felipe** with its white towers to the west of the central park. The **Museo del Ambar** off Calle Duarte, to the west, and the **Mercado** (market) to the south west of the museum.

A visit to the **Brugal Rum Distillery** on Avenida Colon, will give you the opportunity to learn how rum is produced, how the raw material is grown and harvested, and more importantly, what the finished product tastes like! The distillery is open from Monday to Friday between 9am and noon and 2pm to 5pm.

The tourist harbour plays

host to frequent cruise ships, and lies to the west of Fuerte de San Filipe, while the palm-lined Malecon (sea wall) runs eastwards from the fort to Playa Long Beach. As in all Dominican coastal towns, the Malecon is where people gather to stroll, talk or listen to music during the evening. Along its length are food stalls and at night it comes alive with music and the smells of food and people enjoying a stroll beside the ocean. The eastern end of the Malecon tends to be busier.

The Central Square in Independence Park is another popular meeting place with its recently-restored turn of the century gazebo where concerts are often held on Sunday afternoons. There is a Taino museum at Plaza Arawak.

Amber

The Amber Museum in Puerto Plata tells the story of this fascinating and expensive substance. Many people believe that amber is a semi-precious stone, but it is actually the fossilised resin of prehistoric trees, perhaps as many as 40 million years old. The amber mined in the Dominican Republic is some of the most highly sought after because of its quality and colouring. Most amber is yellow with shades of orange and brown, and red amber is very rare and valuable. Because the resin is fossilised, it is not uncommon to find insects, air bubbles or pieces of leaf trapped inside the substance, and these add considerably to its value. Beads of amber can be mounted as stones in jewellery, carved or fused together to create multi-coloured strips of amberoid. The country's amber reserves are not commercially exploited, and although some is exported, most is used by local artists and craftsmen.
The museum has displays showing the many beautiful

A cable car runs from just south of town, which can be taken up to the 2,600 feet (793m) summit of **Montasa Isabel de Torres**. The view from the top is usually magnificent and there is a restaurant and small botanical gardens. The cable car operates daily from 8am to 5pm except Wednesday, although trips may not be as frequent during the summer.

---

ways that amber can be used. There is a craft shop where you can buy amber jewellery. The museum has guided tours in English and is open from Monday to Saturday between 9am and 5pm (☎ 586-2848).

Film director Steven Spielberg visited the town and the amber museum, to research for his film Jurassic Park which features an amber mine.

Playa Dorada

The coast road from Puerta Plata then runs to Playo Dorada. Inland there are huge areas of sugar cane, while the coastal strip is now the main tourist area in the country with hotel after hotel, championship golf courses, attractions and all manner of watersports.

Sugar cane brought to the island by Columbus in 1493 was first planted in this area.

Playa Dorada is yet another fabulous beach along this impressive stretch of coastline. It is very popular and offers a wide range of watersports activities. Most of these are supplied by the large resort hotels along the beach for their guests, but you can often rent equipment or use the facilities if you ask at reception or the beach concessionaire. There is a large choice of restaurants, as well as casinos and an 18-hole golf course designed by Robert Trent Jones. The waterside has been well developed with attractive gardens and bike trails winding past the growing number of hotels. The Playa Dorada Plaza has restaurants, cafes, shops, disco, photo processing, sports centre and a games room. Several new hotels are being built.

Sosúa

Sosúa is 15 miles (24km) to the east, and the most popular beach along the coast. At weekends, the locals turn out in force as well. The town was founded in 1940 by about 600 Jewish refugees, and is really in two separate parts: the tourist section of El Batey, and the traditional residential area of Charamicos on the other side of the bay.

Both communities take great pride in the appearance of their neighbourhoods and there are pretty gardens, tree-lined streets, and attractive buildings.

Because of the hotels and their guests, vendors ply the beach selling wood carvings, arts and crafts, T-shirts and so on. This is a great place to hang out. The beach is beautiful with deep sand and stretches for more than a mile (2km): you can escape to the shade of one of the palms that line the strand, enjoy a drink at one of the many lively beach bars, or linger over a meal in one of the charming little restaurants.

Cabarete

Cabarete has a world famous reputation for its windsurfing. There are onshore winds year round but they are at their best during the winter. It was here in 1987 that the world championships were held, and world champion Mickey Bouwmeester runs a windsurfing centre during the winter. While the sea can be a little choppy, the wide sweeping beach around the bay is magnificent and stretches off into the distance. There are scores of lively bars and restaurants along the waterfront to frequent during the evening.

Nearby is the Costa Azul golf course, originally nine holes and now expanded to 18.

To complete the tour, continue east on Highway 5 past even more splendid and secluded beaches, to connect with Highway 21. Follow this south and then cut across via Tamboril back to Santiago.

4B: The North East and Samana

Again starting from Santiago, this time head east to Licey Al Medio, Moca, Salcedo and Tenares. Take Highway 233 north to connect with Highway 5 running east along the coast to **Rio San Juan,** famous for the Gri Gri Lagoon with its marine caves which can be toured by boat.

Cabrera is just south of Cabo Frances Viejo, and the area has many fine beaches, such as **Playa Grande**, dazzling white and shaded by palms and

Above: *Rio San Juan, Laguna Gri Gri*
Below: *There are many local stalls selling gifts and souvenier's*

coconut trees, and beach restaurants that serve really fresh fish.

The road passes Bahia Escosesa (Scot Bay) and Punta Preciosa (Precious Point) with its own fine beach, and Cabo Francés Viejo (Old French Cape) to **Nagua**, the capital of Maria Trinidad Sánchez province. The town has a number of small restaurants for a refreshment break, and shops where you can buy groceries.

Sanchez

Sanchez stands at the head of the Samaná Peninsula, and is a great base if you are interested in wildlife. For many years it was a busy port because of the terminal of the railway running from San Francisco de Macoris and La Vega to the sea. The town has some interesting old Victorian houses and is a great place to buy fresh shrimps caught in the bay. There is now a new port and the Arroyo Barril airport.

Los Haitises National Park

The area to the south and west make up the Los Haitises National Park, an area of karst and mangrove swamps that teems with birdlife.

Karst is a form of very porous limestone which is easily eroded, and it creates a very special landscape of caves, tunnels and sinkholes. Surface water quickly penetrates the porous rock and then carves out underground streams, which can expand into wide caverns. Often the tops of these caves are worn away and collapse leaving deep sinkholes which fill with water, and these are the most common feature of karst landscapes.

This standing water and the extensive mangrove swamps are the home of scores of species of birds, including heron, ibis, pelican, tern and noddies. Overhead you can spot hawks and other birds of prey, and deep in the swamps you might glimpse the elusive jacana. Trips to the park can be arranged from Samaná.

The Samaná Peninsula

The Samaná Peninsula is worth exploring with a growing number of hotels and good beaches on both north and south coasts, many of them secluded and some only accessible by boat.

The peninsula is stunningly beautiful, with lush green hillsides sloping down to the sea. Small pastel-coloured shacks are scattered around the hillsides or by the water's edge. There are fishing boats pulled up on the beaches along Samaná

> ## Whales
>
> Today the Gulf of Arrows is a great place for whale watching: it is the winter breeding grounds of several hundred humpback whales.
>
> The endangered humpback or baleen whale, grows up to 50 feet (15m) in length. It is easily distinguished by its black upper body, knobbly head and very long, narrow pectoral fins. It is one of the most acrobatic of all the whales and seems to enjoy leaping out of the water, and sometimes doing back flips.
>
> During January and February there are often boat trips out to the breeding grounds, now a protected area about 50 miles (80km) offshore, but the whales often venture closer.

Bay and the fishermen sit under the palms mending their nets and selling their catches.

It is said that when Columbus first sailed into the bay, his ships were attacked by the Indians who filled the air with arrows. Beating a hasty retreat, Columbus called the bay, 'the Gulf of Arrows' (Golfo de las Flechas).

Playa Las Terrenas

Playa Las Terrenas is a small but fashionable resort on the north coast, and has glorious beaches to east and west. It is everyone's idea of a tropical beach with tall, swaying palm trees, and a backdrop of mountains covered in lush vegetation. There are several delightful inns and small hotels, and the resort has something of a French air about it.

To the west is El Cozón beach and offshore is Cayo Ballena (Whale Island) lying among the **Silver Banks,** one of the most extensive reefs in the Caribbean.

Cabo Samaná stands at the end of the peninsula and again has delightful coves and beaches.

Samaná

Samaná, full name Santa Bárbara de Samaná, was originally settled by runaway American slaves. The slaves had made their way to French-controlled Haiti, because slavery was abolished there in 1793 by the new Republican government in Paris, after the French Revolution. When Haiti invaded the western half of the island, the American slaves moved in and settled on the Samaná peninsula.

The town is also the home of President Balaguer, although it has changed enormously over the past few years. The original waterfront with its wooden houses, has been transformed. Most of the buildings have been demolished and replaced by modern concrete structures, while a wide boulevard runs along the water's edge. There are some hotels and the town is lively at night time, but it has not developed as fast as the resorts along the northern coast. There are also some pleasant restaurants specialising in traditional dishes, and it is possible to try treats such as ginger bread, johnny cake and coconut fish.

In fact, the aquaduct in the bay was constructed to supply a hotel planned for an offshore cay, but it was never built. Of interest is La Churcha, a prefabricated tin building which was shipped out from England for the Wesleyan Methodists, now part of the Dominican Evangelical Church.

In the hills inland from Samaná is the Cascada Rio Limon, a waterfall which tumbles more than 160 feet (49m) in a series of cascades.

There is a ferry, usually crowded, across the bay to Sabana de la Mar. There is also a boat from Samaná to the island of **Cayo Levantado** which stands in the bay. It has white sand beaches, lush vegetation and now, a 40 room hotel for those who really want to get away from it all.

For the return journey, retrace the route back to Nagua then head south through El Factor to Castillo on Highway 132. Follow this west to San Francisco de Macoris.

Cut across to join Highway 1 at La Vega, for the drive north back to Santiago.

Eating out in the North and Central Highlands

Cabarete

$$ **Casa Laguna**,
Nanny Estate
(☎ 571-0725).

$$ **Chez Cabarete**,
Nanny Estate
(☎ 571-0789).

Playa Dorada

$$ **El Cupey Gourmet**,
Puerta Plata Village, local, seafood and international
(☎ 320-4012).

$$ **Jade Garden**,
Villas Dorados, Oriental
(☎ 320-3000).

$$-$$$ **La Giralda**,
Flamenco Beach Resort, local,

seafood and international
(☎ 320-3660).

$$-$$$ **La Palma,**
Playa Dorado Hotel, international
(☎ 320-3988).

$$ **Rainbow,**
Heavens, international
(☎ 320-5250).

$$-$$$ **Via Venetto,**
Flamenco Beach Resort, Italian
(☎ 320-5084).

Puerto Plata

$$-$$$ **De Armando,**
Calle Separacion, Seafood, Dominican and international
(☎ 586-3418).

$$ **Jardin Suizo,**
Malecon, salad and daily specials.

$$ **Neptune,**
Puerta Plata Beach, seafood and international
(☎ 586-4243).

$$ **Paco's Bananas,**
Spanish and Dominican and seafood specialities.

$$ **Valther's,** Calle Harmanas Mirabal, great seafood
(☎ 586-2329).

Samaná

$$ **Cafe de Paris,**
Malecon, bistro-style dining
(☎ 538-2488).

$-$$ **Camilo's,**
Samaná, seafood and traditional island dishes.

$$ **Chez Francois,**
great seafood and candlelit dining.

$$ **El Nautico,**
Samaná, seafood and the freshest of fish.

$$-$$$ **El Rincon,**
on the waterfront, Las Terrenas, seafood and Dominican.

$$ **Isla Bonita,**
Italian.

$$-$$$ **Jikaco,**
Las Terrenas, classic French.

San José de las Matas

$$ **El Serrano,**
La Mansión, seafood and international
(☎ 581-0393).

Santiago

$$ **Pez Dorado,**
Calle El Sol, Oriental
(☎ 582-2518).

Sosúa

$$ **Anturios,**
La Esplanada, seafood and continental
(☎ 571-3333).

$$ **Cactus Club,**
Calle Pedro Clisante, Mexican.

$$ **Cafe Atlantico,**
excellent seafood.

Fact File

Arrival, Entry Requirements and Customs

Visitors from North America, Britain and legal residents of all European Union countries are admitted on a valid passport provided their stay is for not longer than 90 days. Other visitors may require visas so check with your travel company.

You may be asked to show a return air ticket, and evidence of pre-arranged accommodation or adequate means of support. An immigration form has to be filled in and presented on arrival. The form requires you to say where you will be staying on the island. If you plan to move around, put down the first hotel you will be staying at. The immigration form is in two parts, one of which is stamped and returned to you in your passport. You must retain this until departure when the slip is retrieved as you check in at the airport.

Having cleared immigration, it is quite usual to have to open your luggage for Customs inspection. If you have expensive cameras, jewellery etc. it is a good idea to travel with a photocopy of the receipt.

There is a U.S.$10 departure tax payable at the airport when leaving.

Emergency Telephone Numbers

The emergency number for police, fire and ambulance is 911 although the operator is unlikely to speak English. If you do not speak Spanish, it is best to contact your hotel where you can explain the problem to someone who speaks English. They can then make further calls as necessary. If you need to contact the police, dial ☎ 682-3000 in Santo Domingo, and ☎ 586-2331 in Puerto Plata, although if you cannot speak Spanish, it will help to have someone who can with you. For an ambulance you can also dial ☎ 567-1101.

A to Z of the Dominican Republic

Accommodation

There is a wide range of accommodation to suit all tastes and pockets, from exclusive resorts and top class hotels to inns, aparthotels, and delightful guest houses, and self-catering apartments, luxury hilltop villas, mountain hideaways and beach cottages.

If you want to eat out and explore quite a lot, it pays to stay in a hotel offering board only. If you want to laze on the beach and not stray far from the hotel, choose a hotel package offering meals as well.

There are also apartments, holiday villas and beach cottages available for short and long rent offering you the privacy of your own accommodation and the flexibility to eat in or out, with cooks and maid service available if required. If travelling in remoter parts of the country it is advisable to book accommodation in advance, and many country hotels and guest houses will only accept pesos. See under Hotels for details.

Airports

Las Américas
(☎ 549-0450)

Herrera, Santo Domingo
(☎ 567-3900)

Gregorio Luperón, Puerto Plata
(☎ 586-0219)

Arroyo Barril, Samaná
Maria Montés, Barahona
Cibao, Santiago
(☎ 582-4894)

Punta Aguila, La Romana
(☎ 556-5565)

Punta Cana, Higney
(☎ 686-8790)

Airlines

APA International Air
(☎ 547-2727)

Aeroméxico
(☎ 541-5151)

Aeropostal
(☎ 566-2334)

Aerotour Airlines
(☎ 227-2575)

Alitalia
(☎ 562-1797)

Air 2000
(☎ 541-5151)

Air France
(☎ 686-8419)

Air Portugal
(☎ 472-1441)

ALM
(☎ 687-4569)

American Airlines
(☎ 542-5151)

Fact File

American Eagle
(☎ 682-9545)

Bávaro Sun Flight
(☎ 685-8411)

Carnival Air Lines
(☎ 563-5300)

Cóndor
(☎ 682-8133)

Continental Airlines
(☎ 541-2000)

Iberia
(☎ 686-9191)

Lufthansa
(☎ 689-9625)

Martinair Holland
(☎ 688-6661)

Puerto Plata
(☎ 320-8246)

Varig
(☎ 565-9151)

Viasa
(☎ 687-2688)

Banks

Most banks are open from Monday to Friday between 8.30am and 3pm or 4.30pm and some branches in tourist areas or large cities are also open on Saturday from 8am to noon. Airport banks usually remain open until the last incoming flight.

Currency

The official currency on the island is the Peso (or Republica Dominicana dollar) RD$, which is divided into 100 centavos with 1,5, 10, 25 and 50 cent coins. There are notes in denominations of 1, 5, 10, 20, 50, 100, 500 and 1,000 pesos. The exchange rate fluctuates but a good rule of thumb is to work on a rate of US$1=RD$13 and £1=RD$20.

Foreign currency can be exchanged for pesos at most banks, major hotels and Banco de Reservas counters at the airports. Keep all receipts, and do not exchange too much money at a time, as it is not always possible to convert surplus pesos back again at the end of your trip. You should be able to do this at the airport on production of an exchange receipt, airport return ticket and passport, but the bank at the airport is not always open.

Resist the temptation to exchange money on the black market. While the deal may sound very advantageous, it is easy to get tricked or worse.

The major credit cards are widely accepted by hotels, tourist restaurants, car hire companies and large stores but are of little use in the country areas where pesos are the only currency.

Always have a few small denomination notes for tips.

Beaches and swimming

There are almost 250 miles (400km) of beautiful beaches: some are in the heart of the main tourist areas with hotels, restaurants and attractions, while others are secluded with no facilities other than glorious sun, sand and sea. Many of the beaches are fringed with tall palms for shade with calm, clear, warm, turquoise seas. The beaches are clean, litter free and seldom crowded.

Northern coast

The main tourist areas are in and to the east of Puerto Plata, and include Playa Dorada which is good for windsurfing, and the popular Sosúa, both offering an impressive range of watersports. Apart from these, there are scores of great beaches both to the east and west: there are lovely beaches at Cofresi, Luperon and the secluded Punta Rucia, north of Villa Isabela, to the west; if you continue east, however, you can find your own secluded bays and coves. Cabarete has a lovely beach and is great for windsurfing, but it is exposed to the onshore winds which can cause tricky swimming conditions. The world championships were held there in 1987. Further east there are lovely beaches around Cabo Frances Viejo and at Playa Grande, just outside Cabrera.

Eastern coast

There are good beaches on the southern shores of the Samaná peninsula around Samaná and opposite at Macao and Miches, but the best are on the northern side on either side of Playa las Terrenas. Local buses run to Playa Las Galeras at the end of the peninsula, and you can take a boat from Samaná to Caya Levantad, which lies about 6 miles (10km) to the east.

There are also many beaches along the coast between Sabana de la Mar and Playa Bavaro. The sandy beaches are spectacular but care is needed when swimming because the waves can be rough and there is often a strong undertow. Playa Bavaro has developed as a tourist resort with several hotels.

Fact File

Southern coast

Most of the best beaches are to the east of Santo Domingo, and include Boca Chica which is very popular – and noisy – with Dominicans from the capital at weekends and public holidays. The next beach area is around Juan Dolio where there are several beaches, then Casa de Campo with the uninhabited Isla Catalina just offshore. You can get a boat across from Casa de Campo.

Try the beaches at Embassy, Guayacanes, La Romana, Bayahibe and Dominicus. There are also lovely beaches around Punta Cana, just south of Cabo Engaso, the most easterly point of the island. In the south west there are good beaches at Bani, Los Patos and Enriquillo.

Tanning safely

The sun is very strong but sea breezes often disguise just how hot it is. If you are not used to the sun, take it carefully for the first two or three days, use a good sun screen with a factor of 15 or higher, and do not sunbathe during the hottest parts of the day. Wear sunglasses and a sun hat. Sunglasses will protect you against the glare, especially strong on the beach, and sun hats will protect your head.

If you spend a lot of time swimming or scuba diving, take extra care, as you will burn even quicker because of the combination of salt water and sun. Calamine lotion and preparations containing aloe are both useful in combating sunburn.

Buses/long distance taxis

For transportation between cities

Taxi Anacaona
(☎ 530-4800)
Emely Tours
(☎ 687-7114)

Metro Servicios Turisticos
(☎ 530-2850)
Transporte Turistico Tanya
(☎ 565-5691)

Car Rental/Driving

Cars, jeeps and other 4 wheel drive vehicles can be hired and provide the best way of exploring the country, although the cost is very expensive and it is cheaper to hire as a group and share the cost. If you plan to go at peak periods, it is best to hire a vehicle in advance through your travel agent. Cars can be hired, however, at airports, hotels or car hire offices on the island.

Because of the cost of new vehicles and servicing them, car hire is expensive and some companies offer you a choice of new or old vehicles.

Hire car rates vary enormously but start from around U.S.$90-100 a day for a newish compact, and from U.S.$50-60 for a car that has seen better days. Jeeps or other four wheel drive vehicles are much more expensive. There is quite a wide range of vehicles available and rates depend both on the type of vehicle and the rental company. There are usually quite a lot of incentives, so it pays to shop around.

To hire a car you must be 25 years old and hold a valid driving licence, but your stay cannot exceed 90 days. An imprint of your credit card is usually required, which acts as a deposit. Most companies require a minimum two-day rental for unlimited mileage, otherwise single day renters usually pay an extra charge based on the miles travelled.

When you pick up the car, check it carefully for dents and scratches and make sure these are logged on the booking form. Also check to make sure the wheels are in good condition, including the spare, and that there is a working jack. If planning to tour the countryside, always try to keep your fuel topped up, as there are not a lot of service stations and those that there are, may be closed.

Drive on the right and stick to the speed limits, even though no one else seems to. The speed limit is 60kph (37mph) in towns, and 80kmp (50 mph) on highways unless otherwise signposted. There are tolls on many main roads and highways but these are only a few pesos depending on the size of vehicle. You will also often come across 'community' road blocks, especially in the countryside, with local people trying to raise money for a local housing project, or even the local fire brigade wanting to get a new piece of equipment. It is up to you whether you give or not, but a small donation will bring big smiles and make you feel good.

Although there are speed limits, even in the countryside many drivers race along at breakneck speeds. They will sit on your bumper until the first opportunity presents itself and

Fact File

then overtake and roar off. While most drivers like to race along, they think nothing of then stopping in the middle of the road to have a chat with another driver or a friend. You may be able to get past, but normally you have to wait until they finish their conversation and the vehicle moves off.

There are lots of scooters and motor cycles to be avoided and it is not uncommon to see up to four people riding on a single scooter.

When driving, exercise caution at all times. In towns, the traffic is often chaotic because most drivers adopt the motto "he who dares, wins". Often the only way to get out into the main flow of traffic is to force your way through. If you wait for someone to stop to let you in, you could be in for a long wait. Traffic lights are often ignored and traffic signs, especially pointing out one way streets, may be difficult to spot or may be non-existent so watch what other vehicles are doing.

Avoid clearly marked 'no parking' zones or you might pick up a ticket.

Driving under the influence of alcohol or drugs is against the law, and there are heavy penalties if convicted, especially if it resulted in an accident.

If you have an accident or breakdown during the day, it is best to call your car hire company, so make sure you have the telephone number with you. They will usually send out a mechanic or a replacement vehicle.

If you are stuck, make sure the car is off the road, lock the vehicle and call a taxi to take you back to your hotel. Report the problem to the car hire company or the police as soon as possible.

It is not unusual to be stopped by the traffic police in rural areas who will check your vehicle in the hope of finding something wrong and levying an on the spot fine – usually only a few pesos.

Some useful signs:

calle sin salida	dead end
carretera cerrada	road closed
cruce de peatones	pedestrian crossing
desprendimiento	landslide
desvio	detour
estacion de peaje	toll booth

no entre	no entry
no estacione	no parking
peligro	danger
transito/una via	one way
zona escolar	school zone

Fact File

Hire companies include:

American International Rent A Car,
Avenida Independencia,
Santo Domingo,
(☎ 6532-0505).

Auto Rental Avis,
Avenida Abraham Lincoln,
Santo Domingo,
(☎ 535-7191).

Budget,
Avenida John F Kennedy,
Santo Domingo,
(☎ 567-0175), and at the airport (☎ 549-0351).

Cima Rent A Car,
Avenida 27 de Febrero 334,
Santo Domingo,
(☎ 565-7005).

Dollar,
Avenida George Washington, Santo Domingo,
(☎ 685-1519).

Hertz,
Avenida Independencia,
Santo Domingo,
☎ 688-2277,
and at the airport
(☎ 549-0454).

Honda Rent A Car, Aveninda John F Kennedy, Santo Domingo,
(☎ 567-1015).

Marlon Rent A Car,
Avenida 27 de Febrero,
Santo Domingo,
(☎ 566-3435).

McDeal Rent A Car, Avenida George Washington, Santo Domingo,
(☎ 688-6518).

Metro,
Winston Churchill, Hatuey
(☎ 544-4580).

National,
Avenida Abraham Lincoln,
Santo Domingo,
(☎ 562-1444).

Nelly Rent A Car,
Avenida José Contreras,
Santo Domingo,
(☎ 535-8800).

Patsy Rent A Car,
Avenida Bolivar, Santo Domingo,
(☎ 686-4333)

Rentauto,
Avenida 27 de Febrero,
Santo Domingo,
(☎ 566-7222).

Thrifty Car Rentals,
Avenida Bolivar, Santo Domingo,
(☎ 685-9191).

Toyota Rent A Car,
Avenida 27 de Febrero,
Santo Domingo,
(☎ 566-7221).

Via Rent A Car,
Avenue John F Kennedy,
Santo Domingo,
(☎ 565-1818).

Churches

About 90 per cent of the population is Roman Catholic and religion exerts a great influence on most aspects of life. Many of the religious ceremonies and practices, especially in rural areas, combine some elements of African belief and traditions.

Clothing

Casual is the keyword but you can generally be as smart or as cool as you like. There are a number of upmarket restaurants and clubs where there are dress codes, and if you plan to visit these, you should pack accordingly. Beachwear is fine for the beach and pool areas, but cover up a little for the street. Informal is the order of the day and night, and this is not the place for suits and ties or evening gowns, unless you really like dressing up for dinner.

During the day, light cotton casual clothes are ideal for exploring. During the evening, a light jumper or wrap may sometimes be needed. It is fun to change for dinner, but for men this normally means smart slacks or trousers, and for women a summer dress or similar. There are establishments, however, where sports coats or jackets are not out of place, and women can be as elegant as they wish.

If you plan to explore on foot, stout footwear and a good waterproof jacket are essential. It is advisable to wear sunglasses and a hat to protect from the sun during the hottest part of the day, and you will need sandals on the beach as the sand can get too hot to walk in bare feet.

Note: Shorts and sleeveless shirts are not permitted in churches, casinos and some restaurants.

Disabled Facilities

Many of the watersports and dive operations will accommodate disabled visitors. There are some facilities for the disabled at most of the larger resorts.

Drugs

There are strict laws prohibiting the possession and use of drugs, including marijuana. Heavy fines and prison await those who ignore the law.

Electricity

The usual electricity supply is 110-120 volts, 60 cycles which is suitable for U.S. appliances. Adaptors are necessary for European appliances without dual voltages. Most large hotels have their own generators because power cuts are quite common –although tourist areas are given priority. It is always wise to pack a candle, matches and have a torch with fresh batteries.

Embassies and Consulates

The Dominican Republic has a large number of embassies and consulates, most of them based in Santo Domingo.
They include:

Canadian Consulate,
Avenida Maximo Gomez,
(☎ 685-1136)

British Consulate,
Avenida Abraham Lincoln,
(☎ 540-3132)

French Embassy,
Avenida George Washington,
(☎ 689-2161)

German Embassy,
Avenida Lope de Vega,
(☎ 565-8811)

Italian Embassy,
Avenida Rodriguez Obijio,
(☎ 689-3684)

United States Embassy,
Avenida César Nicolás Penson
(☎ 221-2171)

Festivals/Public Holidays *

Being a devoutly Catholic country, many of the special holidays celebrated are those of saints and religious festivals. While many countries, however, make do with a single day of celebrations, Dominicans usually manage to extend these, often to several days. Apart from these national holidays, every town has its own patron saint who has to be suitably celebrated.

Fact File

Carnival is the main annual festival and takes place during the week of Independence Day. Other main festivals are Merengue which is held at the end of July and beginning of August in Santo Domingo, and during the second week of October in Puerto Plata.

* public holiday

January

1 January – New Year's Day *
6 January – Epiphany*
21 January – Our Lady of Altagracia Day, the national patron saint*
26 January – Juan Pablo Duarte's Birthday *

February

Ash Wednesday (date varies)
Carnival (during the week of Independence Day)
27 February – Independence Day*

March/April

Good Friday *(date varies)
Easter Monday *(date varies)

May

1 May – Labour Day *

June

Corpus Christ Day * (60 days after Easter, date varies)
5 June – Feast of San Felipe, Puerto Plata
13 June – Feast of San Antonio – Sosúa
29 June – Feast of San Pedro Apostol, San Pedro de Macoris

July

Merengue Festival
22 July – Feast of Santiago Apostol, Santiago
25 July – Feast of San Cristábal, San Cristobal

August

15 August – Feast of Nuestra Seúora de Antigua, La Vega
16 August – Restoration Day*

September

24 September – Nuestra Seúora de las Mercedes, Constanza*

October

4 October – Nuestra Seúora del Rosario, Barahona
24 October – Feast of San Rafael, Boca Chica

November

6 November – Constitution Day

December

4 December – Feast of Santa Barbara, Samaná
25th Christmas Day *
New Year's Eve

Fruits and spices

There is a great variety to be tried and enjoyed. See details under the Food and Drink section in chapter 2.

Gambling

There are about 20 hotels with casinos in the capital or along the south, east and north coasts. They all offer Las Vegas style gambling with blackjack, craps, roulette, slot machines, poker and baccarat. Players must be over the age of 18, and most casinos are open from 4pm until 4am (and often 6am at weekends). Gambling on horse racing and cockfighting is also popular.

Health

As a result of problems with food hygiene and sanitation in 1997/8, the Government and tour operators responded quickly and introduced a monitoring system for food preparation, food management hygiene and water quality. Nonetheless, it is recommended that visitors take sensible precautions such as drinking bottled water and obtaining the appropriate innoculations. These are currently: Hepatitis A and Polio. Typhoid is also necessary for those planning up-country excursions where conditions can be unsanitary, infectious and parasitic diseases are common, and health services are restricted. If you are arriving from an infected area, a Yellow Fever certificate is required.

There are 24 hour emergency rooms in:
Santo Domingo – Clinica Abreu, Calle Beller (☎ 688-4411) and Clinica Gomez Patiso, Avenida Independencia (☎ 685-9131).

Santiago – Hospital José Cabral y Baez, Avenida Central (☎ 583-4311).

Puerto Plata – Centro Médico Dr Bourigal, Antera Mota (☎ 586-2342), Hospital Ricardo Limardo, J.F. Kunhart (☎ 586-2210), Centro Medico, Máximo Gómez (☎ 221-0171).

La Romana – Centro Médico Oriental, Sta. Rosa (☎ 556-25550).

Fact File

Hotels

Prices quoted by hotels are for rooms, whether one or two people are sharing, and you may find it difficult to get a reduction if you are travelling alone, but have a go. Some terms: MAP stands for Modified American Plan i.e. breakfast and dinner are included. EP or European Plan means bed only and no meals, and AP for American Plan, means room and all meals. $ represents inexpensive accommodation, $$ moderate, and $$$ de-luxe.

Santo Domingo

Acuarium Hotel
Calle Isableita
(☎ 595-6755)
58 good value rooms with swimming pool and meeting rooms $-$$

Caribeso Hotel
(☎ 685-3167)
106 rooms with pool $-$$

Commercial Hotel
(☎ 682-8161)
a good value 75 room property $-$$

Continental Hotel
Maximo Gomez Avenida
(☎ 689-1151)
A three star city centre hotel with 100 rooms and suites with balcony and ocean view. It has a restaurant, disco and pool. $$

Delta Hotel
(☎ 535-7222)
73 rooms with swimming pool $-$$

Dominican Fiesta Hotel
Avenida Anancaona
(☎ 562-8222)
316 rooms, including the Club Miguel Executive Floor, with pool, tennis, casino and conference facilities $$-$$$

El Embajador Hotel and Casino
Avenida Sarasota
(☎ 221-2131)
316 rooms, including the Club Miguel Executive Floor, plus 3 restaurants, bars, nightclub, with pool, jacuzzi, shopping area, beauty parlour, tennis, casino and conference facilities $$-$$$

El Napolitano Hotel and Casino
Avenida George Washington
(☎ 687-1131)
72 rooms with coffee shop, restaurant, nightclub, entertainment, pool and conference facilities $-$$

Fact File

Hispaniola and Casino
Avenida George Washington (Malecon)
(☎ 221-1511)
A conveniently located hotel with 165 rooms and suites, with 2 restaurants, bar, disco, pool, tennis, fitness centre, shops and casino $$

Hostal Nicolas de Ovando
Calle de las Damas
(☎ 687-3101)
A delightful 45-room hotel in the heart of the Colonial City set in a 16th century former Governor's palace, with spacious rooms set around three cool, tiled courtyards and pool. Good restaurant $$

Hostal Nicolas Nader
Calle Luperon
(☎ 687-6674)
In the Colonial City and still with a wonderful, quiet, old world charm. The historic building set around its inner courtyard has 10 comfortable rooms. There is a bar and a wide choice of restaurants nearby $$

Hotel Aida
Calle Espaillat, (☎ 685-7692)
Good value, comfortable rooms, $

Hotel Bolivar
Avenida Bolivar
(☎ 685-2200)
Restaurant, bar and first class service (hotel industry training school) $

Hotel Cervantes
Avenida Cervantes
(☎ 686-8161)
180 rooms 24 hour restaurant, bars, swimming pool, entertainment and conference facilities. $-$$

Hotel Comodoro
Avenida Bolivar
(☎ 541-2277)
87 rooms with coffee shop, restaurant, disco, entertainment, swimming pool and conference facilities $-$$

Hotel Continental
Avenida Máximo Gómez
(☎ 689-1151)
100 rooms with coffee shop, restaurant, nightclub, entertainment, swimming pool and conference facilities $-$$

Renaissance Jaragua Hotel
Avenida George Washington (Malecon)
(☎ 221-2222)
A luxury 310-room city hotel close to all the action and providing a lot of its own, with 10 restaurants and lounges, casino, ballroom, nightclub, tennis centre, swimming pool with waterfalls, European spa and conference facilities $$$

Naco Hotel and Casino
Tiradentes
(☎ 562-3100)
106 rooms with coffee shop, restaurant, pool, sauna, entertainment, casino and conference facilities $-$$

Fact File

Plaza Colonial Apart-Hotel
(☎ 687-9111)
90 rooms with pool and meeting rooms $-$$

Plaza Florida Apart-Hotel
Avenida Bolivar
(☎ 541-3957)
32 apartments with coffee shop, restaurant, disco and pool $$

Royal Hotel
(☎ 686-1717)
64 rooms with pool and meeting rooms $-$$

San Gerónimo Hotel
(☎ 535-1000)
80 rooms with pool and casino $-$$

Santo Domingo Hotel
Avenida George Washington (Malecon)
(☎ 221-1511)
An upmarket hotel with 220 rooms, catering for both the tourist and business traveller. It has three restaurants, bars, swimming pool, floodlit tennis, fitness centre, sauna and massage, casino and conference facilities. $$$

Sheraton Santo Domingo
George Washington Avenue
(☎ 221-6666)
Overlooking the Caribbean with 260 rooms with 3 restaurants (Antoine-international, La Canasta-island specialities and La Terraza - pool terrace), bars, disco, pool, floodlit tennis, health club with separate gyms for men and women, and sauna, casino and conference facilities and business centre. Honeymoon packages available.$$$

V Centenario Inter-Continental
Avenida George Washington (Malecon)
(☎ 221-0000)
De-luxe 201 room hotel with swimming pool, tennis and casino $$$

Outside the capital

Barahona

Barahona Beach Club
(☎ 685-5184)
Suites and apartments with riding, tennis and watersports $$

Casa Bonita
Bahoruca
(☎ 685-5184)
A lovely, intimate hillside country inn overlooking the mountains and sea. It has six cottage style buildings with typical Criolla thatched roofs set in landscaped gardens. It has restaurant, bar, pool and offers nearby horse riding, snorkelling with eco-tours, bike and jeep hire and private beach $$.

Hotel Guayocura
(☎ 685-6161)
Comfortable, budget accommodation $

Riviera Beach Hotel
Avenida Enriquillo
(☎ 221-2131)
105 rooms with coffee shop, restaurant, sauna, swimming pool, tennis, beach, entertainment and conference facilities $-$$

Boca Chica
Boca Chica
(☎ 563-2200)
A 273 room resort with coffee shop, restaurant, disco, pool, tennis, golf, beach, entertainment and conference facilities $$$

Villa Sans Soucy
(☎ 523-4461)
A 17 room property with coffee shop, restaurant, pool, golf and beach $-$$

Cabarete
Auberge du Roi Tropicale
(☎ 571-0770)
The home of the Micky Bouwmeester windsurfing school, with restaurant, swimming pool, a wealth of other water sports and health centre. $-$$

Casa Laguna
(☎ 571-0725)
Close to the beach with restaurant, lovely gardens, swimming pool, and watersports $$

Nanny Estate
(☎ 571-0744)
Apartment villas with restaurant, swimming pool $$

Punta Goleta Beach Resort
(☎ 571-0701)
A 250 room all inclusive resort set in 100 acres (40 hecatres) of tropical gardens with restaurant, nightclub, pool, sauna, tennis, golf and entertainment. Honeymoon packages available $$-$$$

Constanza
Hotel Nueva Suizza
(☎ 539-2233)
60 rooms, great mountain views $$

Costambar
Bayside Hill Resort and Beach Club
(☎ 586-5260)
150 rooms with coffee, shop, restaurant, nightclub, entertainment, sauna, swimming pool, beach, tennis, golf, casino and conference facilities $$

Higney/Playa Bavaro/ Punta Cana

Caribbean Village Bávaro
(☎ 687-5747)
A 540 room resort with restaurant, disco, pool, tennis, beach, sauna, entertainment and conference facilities $$$

Club Mediterrané
(☎ 567-5228)
A 340 room resort with coffee shop, restaurant, disco, pool, tennis, beach,

Fact File

Fact File

entertainment and conference facilities $$-$$$

Punta Cana Beach Resort
(☎ 541-2262/221-2262)
Set in 100 acres (40 hectares) of tropical gardens with 400 rooms, 5 restaurants, coffee shop, disco, swimming pool and swim up bar, tennis, beach, watersports, entertainment and conference facilities $$

Jarabacoa

Pinar Dorado
(☎ 689-5105)
A comfortable, good value double rooms $

River Resort
(☎ 574-2918)
The accommodation is in delightful cabins on the hillside $$

Juan Dolio

Caribbean Village Costa Linda
(☎ 526-2161)
A 162-room and villa resort with restaurant, pool, beach, entertainment and casino $$

Diamond Costa Caribe
(☎ 526-2244)
313 rooms on the beach. An all-inclusive resort with restaurant, pool, beach, sauna, entertainment and casino $$-$$$

Metro Country Club
Golf special, 18 hole par 72 "Los Marlins" course.
Metro is located adjacent to many of the first class hotels in the Juan Dolio area.
Golf academy employs profesionals to instruct both beginners and advanced players.
Golf packages available.

Metro Hotel and Marina
(☎ 526-2811)
A 223 room property with coffee shop, restaurants, disco, Olympic-size pool, tennis, golf, horse riding, beach, sauna, watersports, private marina, sailing, fishing, entertainment and conference facilities $$-$$$

Playa Real
(☎ 221-2131)
A new hotel with 225 beach side rooms, and being expanded to 400. It has coffee shop, restaurant, pool, swimming, tennis, golf, beach, entertainment and conference facilities $$-$$$

Renaissance Capella Beach Resort
San Pedro de Macoris - Santo Domingo Road
(☎ 526-1080)
A five star 283 room beachside property with excellent facilities and entertainment programmes for adults and children. Casino.
$$-$$$

Posada Inn
Altos de Chavón
(☎ 523-3333)
Ten luxury rooms with swimming pool and great views $$-$$$

Luperon
Caribbean Village Luperon
(☎ 571-8303)
An all inclusive 300 room resort with restaurant, nightclub, pool, tennis, beach and entertainment $$$

Playa Dorada
Caribbean Village Club
(☎ 320-1111)
332 rooms with all inclusive plans available, with restaurant, disco, pool, tennis, golf, beach, sauna and entertainment $$-$$$

Dorado Naco Suite Resort
(☎ 320-2019)
200 one and two bedroom apartments, with coffee shop, Flamingo gourmet restaurant, pool, golf, tennis, scuba, watersports, horse riding, sauna, entertainment and conference facilities and nearby casino $$

AMHSA Heavens
(☎ 320-5250)
A 150 room lively club-style resort with coffee shop, restaurant, disco, pool, gym, golf, beach, sauna and lots of entertainment and activities $$-$$$

Occidental Flamenco Beach Resort
(☎ 320-5084)
A 582 room resort with all inclusive option, coffee shop, restaurant, pools, tennis, golf, beach, sauna, entertainment and conference facilities $$$

Playa Dorado Hotel
(☎ 320-3988)
A 254 room resort with coffee shop, restaurant, disco, pool, tennis, golf, beach, entertainment, casino, and conference facilities $$-$$$

The Princess Golf, Tennis and Beach Resorts
A large 336-room resort with a wide range of sports facilities, with restaurants, and nightly entertainment $$$

Puerto Plata
Hostal Jimesson
Avenida John F Kennedy
(☎ 586-2177)
A charming 22 room hotel $-$$

Riu Merengue
A 780-bed property at Maimón, just to the west

Punta Rucia
$$-$$$ **Discovery Bay Club**
(☎ 562-7475)
All inclusive 29 room resort with restaurant, pool, beach and entertainment

Fact File

Fact File

Orquideria del Sol
(☎ 583-2825)
Small 28 room hotel set in gardens with many kinds of orchid, and overlooking the beach

Samaná Peninsula

Caribbean Village Playa Grande
(☎ 582-1170)
A 300 room property with restaurant, nightclub, pool, tennis, beach and entertainment $$$

Cayacoa Beach Resort,
Las Terrenas/Sanchez
(☎ 538-3131)
A 80 rooms and suites in the hills overlooking the bay, and set in a lovely park and gardens, with coffee shop, restaurant, pool, tennis, beach and entertainment $$

Cayo Levantado Beach Resort
Las Terrenas/Sanchez
Set on its own island in the bay, has 44 rooms with coffee shop, restaurant, pool, tennis, beach and entertainment $$-$$$

El Portillo Beach Club
(☎ 688-5715)
171 rooms and cabins set in the tropical gardens which overlook the beach and offshore reef, with restaurant, disco, pool, tennis, watersports and entertainment $$$

Hacienda
A small very friendly property with 5 rooms $-$$

Hotel Restaurant Dinny
(☎ 589-9539)
Good value, in-town budget accommodation $

Hotel Tropic Banana
(☎ 566-5941)
Lively hotel with 30 rooms scattered around the tropical gardens and swimming pool, popular and usually live music afternoon and evening $-$$

Moorea Beach Hotel
Las Galeras Beach
(☎ 689-4105)
12 comfortable rooms and restaurant $$

Tropical Lodge Hotel
Samaná, (☎ 538-2480) $

San José de las Matas

Club Spa La Mansión
(☎ 581-0393/221-2131)
270 rooms with coffee shop, restaurant, pool, sauna, tennis, entertainment and conference facilities $$

Sosúa

Casa Marina Beach Club
Calle Dr Alejo Martinez, El Batey
(☎ 571-3690)
On its beach in the tourist quarter, with 344 rooms, 3 restaurants, 2 pools, beach, jacuzzi and entertainment $-$$

One Ocean Place
(☎ 571-3131)

Sand Castle Resort
(☎ 530-1684)
The ornate Spanish-style all-inclusive resort is set on the cliffs with its own private beach, with 240 rooms, coffee shop, Venezia, El Guarapo and El Sahara gourmet restaurants, bar, swimming pool, beach, disco, tennis, horse riding, cycles, watersports, kids club, entertainment and conferencefacilities. Honeymoon packages available $$-$$$

Sea Breeze
(☎ 571-2115)
A small 31 room property in El Batey with coffee shop, restaurant, disco, pools, beach, scuba and diving lessons and entertainment $

Tropix Hotel
(☎ 571-2291)
A small, comfortable and friendly with 10 rooms set in pretty garden, dining room and swimming pool $

Yaroa Hotel
Calle Dr Roson,
(☎ 571-2651) $

Guest Houses, Villas and Apartments

Hotel La Residence
Santo Domingo $
(☎ 682-4178)

La Mansion Guest House
Santo Domingo $
(☎ 682-2033)

Don Paco Guest House
Boca Chica
(☎ 523-4816)

El Cheverón,
Boca Chica
(☎ 523-4333)

Important things to pack

Sun block cream, sunglasses, sun hat, camera (and lots of film), insect repellant, binoculars if interested in bird watching and wildlife, and a small torch and candle in case of power failures.

Irritating insects

Mosquitoes are not much of a problem on or near the beaches because of onshore winds, but they may well bite you as you enjoy an open air evening meal or lie in bed at night. Use a good insect repellant, particularly if you are

Fact File

planning trips inland. Lemon grass can sometimes be found growing naturally, and a handful of this in your room is also a useful mosquito deterrent. More effective are mosquito coils which burn all night, or even a mosquito net if you are particularly sensitive.

Sand flies can be a problem on the beach. Despite their tiny size they can give you a nasty bite. Make sure you check the ground carefully before sitting down in case there is an ants nest – the bites can itch for days.

Language

The official language spoken is Spanish, although English is widely spoken in hotels and tourist areas. A French patois is spoken by some Haitian immigrants, and many Taino words still exist. Very few people speak English away from the tourist areas, and if do not speak the language and are planning to explore the island, it will pay to learn as many basic words as possible in advance and take a phrase book with you. Road signs are in Spanish (see car hire), and outside tourist areas, menus tend to be only in Spanish

If asking for directions in the country, you are often told "alli mismo", which means "just over there", be don't let that fool you. It is a general term which means the place you are heading for could be anything from a few hundred yards to five or six miles away.

Lost Property

Report lost property as soon as possible to your hotel or the nearest police station.

Mail

The Dominican public postal service has more than 190 offices throughout the country and sending mail both internally and internationally is very cheap, especially when compared with Europe.

Media

There are nine Spanish language national morning and evening newspapers, including the El Caribe, founded in 1948 and Listin Diario, founded in 1889, and both published in Santo Domingo. The others are El Nuevo Diario, El Siglo, El Sol, Hoy, El Nacional, La Noticia and Ultima Hora. English language papers include Bohio Dominicano, the weekly Santo Domingo News and Hispaniola Business. Most leading US and international newspapers and magazines are available in main population centres and tourist areas.

The country has more than 200 radio stations, many of which feature American music. There are 6 television stations plus cable and satellite which provides access to more than 40 U.S. and European channels including all the major American networks.

Museums

There is usually a modest admission charge to visit museums, and most exhibits are labelled in both English and Spanish. Some museums also have a dress code with admission refused for inappropriate wear. This is especially the case if visiting the Cathedral and other religious monuments.

National Parks

The national park system includes both recreational areas incorporated in urban parks and natural areas and scientific reserves in the countryside.

Recreational areas include: National Aquarium, Botanic Gardens, National Zoo, Southern Mirador and Easter Mirador all in Santo Domingo. La Vega Vieja in La Vega, and the Archaeology Park in La Isabela, Puerto Plata. The main national parks consist of: Armando Bermúdez, José del Carmen Ariza, Parque Naçional del Este, Los Haitises, Isla Cabritos, Sierra de Bahoruco, Montecristi and Jaragua.

Fact File

Nightlife

There is a great choice of entertainment from great dining to live theatre and comedy clubs, and karaoke bars to cabaret. Many of the larger hotels and resorts offer live entertainment, and there are bars, dancing and discos. And, for something really exciting, experience an underwater night dive.

Discos and nightclubs include:

Bachata Rose
(☎ 687-6674)

Barra Uno
(☎ 547-2527)

Boncherie
(☎ 472-1603)

Café Atlántico
(☎ 565-1841)

Café Capri
(☎ 566-3679)

Cafezinho
(☎ 567-7262)

Cervantes Piano Bar
(☎ 686-8161)

El Napolitano
(☎ 687-1131)

El Yarey
(☎ 221-6666)

Euro Club
(☎ 541-6226)

Fiesta
(☎ 221-2222)

Guácara Taina
(☎ 530-2666)

Hollywood Cafe
(☎ 66-3349)

Júbilee
(☎ 221-2222)

Las Palamas
(☎ 221-1511)

Merengue Bar
(☎ 221-2222)

Museo del Jamón
(☎ 688-9644)

Neón
(☎ 221-7111)

Omni
(☎ 221-6666) and Steak House
(☎ 549-5505)

Personal Insurance and Medical Cover

Make sure you have adequate personal insurance and medical cover. If you need to call out a doctor or have medical treatment, you will probably have to pay for it at the time, so keep all receipts so that you can reclaim on your insurance.

Pets

If travelling with a pet (cat or dog), a health certificate issued no more than 15 days prior to arrival must be presented, together with proof that the animal has been vaccinated against rabies in the previous 30 days. Dogs also need a parvo-virus vaccine. If these conditions are not met, the animal will be quarantined for up to 30 days.

Pharmacies

There are a number of pharmacies in all main towns and tourist areas and generic drugs are usually available. If specific medication is required, it is best to bring enough for your trip plus a letter from your doctor explaining what is prescribed and why it is needed, in case emergencies supplies become necessary.

Photography

The intensity of the sun can play havoc with your films, especially if photographing near water or white sand. Compensate for the brightness, otherwise your photographs will come out over exposed and wishy washy. The heat can actually damage film so store reels in a box or bag in the hotel fridge if there is one. Also remember to protect your camera if on the beach, as a single grain of sand is all it takes to jam your camera.

It is very easy to get 'click happy', but be tactful and polite when taking photographs. Many islanders are shy or simply fed up with being photographed. You will have to decide whether the picture is worth it, but if a person declines to have their photograph taken, don't ignore this. The islanders are a warm and very hospitable race and if you stop and spend some time finding out what they are doing, they will usually then allow you to take a photograph.

Note: Taking photographs in some museums and military areas is forbidden.

Post Office

The main post office in Santo Domingo is at Centro de los Heroes (☎ 534-6218).

Fact File

Public Toilets

There are not many public toilets on the island, but bars, restaurants and hotels have private facilities which can usually be used if you ask politely.

Restaurants

There is a remarkably large choice when it comes to eating out on the island. There are the inevitable fast food burger, pizza and fried chicken outlets, beach cafes offering excellent value for the money, and elegant upmarket dining rooms, as well as restaurants offering a wide range of ethnic cuisines, from Caribbean cooking to Chinese, Spanish to South American, and Mexican to Japanese. Dominican cuisine is a blend of native Amerindian, Spanish, Middle Eastern and African ingredients and styles.

Most accept credit cards and during peak times of the year, reservations are recommended. If you come across a restaurant not listed in the guide, or have comments about any of those that are, I would very much like to hear from you.

People tend to dine much later than in other countries because of the long siesta and the fine evenings which generally make eating out of doors such a pleasure.

Some restaurants are closed on Saturday for lunch and all day Sunday, but hotel restaurants are open daily and welcome non residents. The restaurants listed in the itineraries are classified by price – $ inexpensive, $$ moderate, $$$ expensive.

Security

It makes sense like anywhere else, not to walk around wearing expensive jewellery or flashing large sums of money. Secure your valuables as you should anywhere, and do not leave items unattended on the beach or in an unlocked car.

Don't carry around your passport, travellers cheques or all your money. Keep them secure in your room or in a hotel safety deposit box. It is also a good idea to have photocopies of the information page of your passport, your air ticket and holiday insurance policy. All will help greatly if the originals are lost.

Dominicans are genuinely warm and friendly and very laid back, so there is little hard selling and they will go to great lengths to make your visit memorable.

The exception to this is in Santo Domingo and the more popular tourist areas, where you are likely to be accosted by touts and hustlers, offering you anything from exclusive guided tours to black market money exchange and drugs. They can be both persuasive and persistent, but be polite and firm: say no and walk on.

Women are generally quite safe, although they may well be propositioned by the macho Dominican males. Again, it pays to be polite but firm, and simply say thanks but no thanks. It is a good idea, however, not to go out unescorted late at night.

Note: You will see a lot of firearms everywhere. The police and military are armed and most businesses, hotels, banks and so on employ private security guards who also carry weapons. Remember that these people are there for your protection.

Service Charges and Taxes

There is a Government tax of 10 per cent on accommodation and 8 per cent on restaurant bills, and a 10 to 15 per cent service charge may also be added to restaurant bills. Menus and tariffs sometimes include these charges so check to make sure they have not been added again. In some shops, such as duty free stores, the price on the label is what you pay, in others it is worth trying to haggle and see how much you can get the price reduced.

Sex

Prostitutes ply their trade openly, and often brazenly, but there is always the danger of sexually transmitted diseases, and cases of HIV are increasing.

Shells

Shells are washed up on to the beaches but they should be left for others to enjoy. Live shells may not be taken by collectors.

Fact File

Shopping

Shopping is fun because of the exchange rates, and there are many great bargains to be had. Shops tend to open at 9am until noon and then close for a long lunch and siesta, opening again at 2pm or 2.30 pm until 7pm. Bartering is a way of life, and you should always bargain to try to get the price of any purchase reduced.

The Dominican Republic has a wide range of shopping from duty-free stores with top name designer clothes, to fine china and crystal, perfumes and jewellery, to island goods such as arts and crafts, handprints, paintings, and spices.

The main shopping area is Santo Domingo which has large shopping malls and big name stores, although all cities and towns have their own smaller shopping centres. Main shopping areas in Santo Domingo are Plaza Central, Plaza Naco, Mercado Modelo (flea market) and along Mella and Conde Streets.

There is duty free shopping at Las Americas and Puerto Playa airports, as well as at a number of locations in Santo Domingo, but goods purchased have to be paid for in U.S. dollars and must be claimed at the airport prior to departure.

Best buys are island arts and crafts and island jewellery featuring amber and larimar. Wicker, rattan and wood furniture is good if you can get it home, while smaller best buys include hand-painted masks, pottery, ceramics, woven articles, paintings by local artists, beautiful hand-made dolls, fashions from local designers, local coffee, rum and beer.

Siesta

The siesta is a way of life and a tradition that has great benefits. It allows you to rest through the hottest part of the day, recover from a good lunch and re-charge the batteries for the evening ahead. Most shops and offices close from 12.20pm to 2.30pm.

Sightseeing and tours

Sightseeing and island tours by land or sea can be organised through hotels, tour representatives or one of the many specialist tour companies. There are organised tours to all

Fact File

the main sights, as well as historical tours of the Colonial City, excursions to other resort areas, and lively tours to enjoy Santo Domingo's nightlife without having to worry about driving.

These include:

Agencia de Viajes u Turismo,
ACN Pension 38,
Santo Domingo,
(☎ 688-3767)

Apolo Tours,
Puerto Plata,
(☎ 586-5329)

Arbaje Tours,
(☎ 535-4941)

Bibi Travels, Jose Contreras,
98, Santo Domingo,
(☎ 532-7141)

Cafemba Tours,
Playa Dorada,
(☎ 320-3969)

Daytours,
Santo Domingo,
(☎ 473-6010)

Domitur,
Santo Domingo,
(☎ 570-7313)

Dorado Travel,
(☎ 686-1067)

Ecoturista,
(☎ 221-4104)

El Dorado Travel,
Santo Domingo,
(☎ 688-6661)

Emely Tours,
Santo Domingo,
(☎ 687-7114)

Fantasy Tours,
(☎ 565-5014)

Go Caribic,
Puerto Plata,
(☎ 586-4075)

Metro Tours,
Avenida Winston Churchill,
Santo Domingo,
(☎ 544-5014)

Mundi Tours,
SAG Meija Ricart 71,
Santo Domingo,
(☎ 562-5025)

Omni Tours,
Santo Domingo
(☎ 565-6591)

Prieto Tours,
Santo Domingo,
(☎ 685-0102),
and Puerto Plata,
(☎ 586-3988)

Puerto Plata Tours,
Beller 70,
(☎ 586-3858)

Sombrero Tours,
Avenida Bolivar 356,
Santo Domingo,
(☎ 688-7573)

Tanya Tours,
Santo Domingo,
(☎ 563-4076)

Thomas Tours,
Santo Domingo,
(☎ 541-4994)

Fact File

Transtours,
Avenida 27 de Febrero,
Santo Domingo,
(☎ 687-9094)

Tropical Tours,
La Romana,
(☎ 566-2512)

Turinter,
Leopoldo Navarro 4,
Santo Domingo,
(☎ 686-4020)

Viajes Barcelo,
Santo Domingo
(☎ 685-8411)

Viajes Bohio,
Santo Domingo,
(☎ 686-7227)

World Travel Centre,
Avenida Lope de Vega,
Santo Domingo,
(☎ 540-2308)

Sport

Baseball

Baseball is the national sport, largely because of the U.S. occupation between 1916 and 1924, and there is a very competitive professional winter league, which often attracts big name U.S. players between late October and January.

Many summer tournaments are also staged and all 26 U.S. baseball clubs have academies or camps in the Dominican Republic on the look out for talent. The Dominican Republic has more than 50 of its best players playing as professionals in North American Leagues. There are stadiums in Santo Domingo, San Pedro de Macoris, La Romana, Puerto Plata, San Francisco de Macoris and Santiago.

Spectator sports include baseball, horseracing, boxing, basketball, volleyball, international windsurfing, powerboat and sailing competitions, motorcycle and car racing.

Santo Domingo boasts the V Centenario Race Track, the Sebelen Bowling Center (built to host the 1997 Panamerican Bowling Games), Quisqueya Baseball Park and its newest sporting complex, Gimnasio-Coliseo de Boxeo, set to become a major venue for world title fights.

Cockfighting

This is very popular and is followed passionately throughout the country, although officially now frowned on by the authorities. There are a number of arenas, especially in country areas, and the main venue in the capital is the

Coliseo Gallistico de Santo Domingo in Avenida Luperón
(☎ 565-3844)

Cycling

Bikes are a good way of getting around and getting a tan, and cycles can be hired at a number of locations in the main cities and resort areas.

Fishing

Fishing is an island pursuit, and many islanders will fish for hours from harbour walls, from the beach or river side.

There is year-round world-class deep sea and game fishing for Atlantic blue marlin, skipjack, the fighting sailfish, blackfin and yellowfin tuna (also called allison), wahoo and white marlin, which can all weigh over 100lbs each. The Mona Passage regularly yields record breaking fish.

Snapper, bonefish, permit, pompano, tarpon, grouper, bonito and barracuda can all be caught close to shore. Around the reefs there is an abundance of grouper, jack crevalle, mutton snapper and yellowtail snapper. Dorado is usually called dolphin (not the mammal but the fish also called mahi-mahi).

Boca de Yuma hosts an annual sport fishing tournament, and there is excellent fishing off Monte Cristi which hosts several annual tournaments.

There are many guides and charter boats for hire. Prices vary enormously depending on the vessel, number of lines allowed and facilities offered.

Fishing charter boats can be found at Boca de Yuma, Boca Chica and Samaná.

Fitness Gyms/Health Centres

Many of the main hotels and resorts offer health and fitness facilities.

Golf

There are sixteen golf courses throughout the country, four more under construction as we went to print, and several more planned.

The top courses are Casa de Campo's three championship 18-hole courses all designed by Peter Dye. The par-72

Fact File

Teeth of the Dog, which fronts the sea on seven holes, was ranked as the 20th best golf course in the world by Golf Magazine. The Links is a par-71 championship course, and the newest and perhaps the most demanding is La Romana Country Club, a private membership club. The courses host a number of annual championships including the annual Casa de Campo Open and the Juan Marichal Golf Classic.

Most courses are situated on or close to major hotels and resorts, such as the Playa Dorada Golf Course on the north coast, designed by Robert Jones Trent. This par-72 18-hole course is within the Playa Dorada resort complex and shared by 15 resorts, although there is usually no problem getting to the tee. The 9-hole Costa Azul course is east of Puerto Plata and Sosúa, and there is another 9-hole course in Costambar, west of Playa Dorada. This course expands to 18-holes with the recent completion of a new 9-hole course at Los Mangos, where there is a pro shop and other amenities.

On the eastern coast the Bávaro Resort has an 18-hole course designed by Juan Manual Gordillo. The par-72 course is flat but tricky to play because of the wind. A new 18-hole course is being built to serve the Punta Cana area. Designed by Robert Trent Jones, it runs beside the beach.

The Santa Domingo Country Club is the capital's premier course. The 18-hole course is open to non-members on weekdays and arrangements can be made directly with the club or through most hotels. It is a very challenging course. The Cayacoa Country Club is only 20 minutes or so from the city, and is less crowded. Apart from the 18-hole course, there is a also tennis, swimming pool, restaurant and bar, as well as a golf academy with private lessons available. The course was originally designed by Pete Dye but has been modified since. It is a spread out, scenic course set in hilly terrain.

Close to Cayacoa is the Lomas Linda Golf Course, a par-3, nine-hole course.

Serving the south east there is the new San Andrés Golf and Country Club in Boca Chica, and the Metro Country Club has completed the first nine holes of a planned 18 hole course in Juan Dolio.

The 18-hole Las Aromas Golf Club is a private members club in Santiago, but day members are welcomed.

In Samaná in the east, is the 9-hole Loma de Chivo Country Club course at the Gran Bahia Hotel. This is the areas first course and is open to the public. Jarabacoa in the mountains has a 9-hole course, and in Bonai, north west of the capital, the Falconbridge Dominicana Mining Company has a short 9-hole course mainly for employees and guests.

The Central Bank is building a new 18-hole course at Playa Grande which is modelled on the famous Pebble Beach. The Robert Trent Jones course should be open in 1997.

Hiking

There are some spectacular walks around the coast and inland, especially in the national parks. Walking is great fun and there are lots of trails, but take stout, non-slip footwear and a waterproof. Protect yourself against insects, carry adequate drinking water and keep an eye on the time, because night falls quickly and you don't want to be caught out on the trail after dark.

Horseback Racing, Riding and Polo

It is one of the few Caribbean islands where you can hire trained polo ponies, while the Hipodromo V Cenenario, Santo Domingo, which opened in the summer of 1995, attracts thoroughbreds from throughout the Caribbean and Central America. (☎ 687-6060)

Jogging

There are jogging tracks at the Olympic Centre, and you can run safely in most green areas and along the Malecón, Paseo de los Indios, and Avenida Mirador del Sur.

Parasailing

Contact Actividades Acuáticas, Boca Chica (☎ 523-4511), Playa Dorada (☎ 320-2567)

Scuba/diving

The waters offer fabulous diving as the island surrounded by pristine reefs, some of them easily accessible from the shore, especially off the south east coast around Punta Cana. The eastern coast offers a stronger swell for windsurfing and surfing, but the seas can sometimes be very rough and care is needed; the west coast beaches offer safe swimming.

There are dive schools in many hotels and resorts where you can learn how to scuba, and there are dive sites to

Fact File

accommodate all levels of experience. There are dive shops in Santo Domingo that organise tours and rent or sell equipment. Many professional scuba schools offer dive packages and guided excursions, as well as training from basic certification to advanced level.

The waters are warm and remarkably clear with excellent visibility. The reefs are easily accessible and they teem with different corals and marine life. There are about 400 shipwrecks in territorial waters, and many of the reefs and wrecks are close to the shore, while there are walls, drop-offs, caves and tunnels to explore in deeper waters.

Best dive sites include:

Isla Catalina, off La Romana, with a good wall dive for experienced divers. The dive site is a 20 minute boat ride from La Romana, and is one of the few inshore places where large numbers of large fish can be seen. The shallower dive is in 25 to 30 feet (8 to 9m) of water to a coral garden with purple sea fans, gorgonias and multi-coloured fish. Further down at between 90 and 100 feet (27 and 30m) there are shoals of near-fluorescent fish.

Bayahibe is a two hour drive from Santo Domingo, and the dive site has become known as the "feeding ground" because large numbers of fish gather there to be fed by the divers.

Saona Island off the south east coast can only be reached by boat from La Romana.

Punta Cana is a relatively new diving area and includes the longest coral reef around the island which is 18.6 miles (30km) long, as well as a number of dive sites for beginners. There are also reef cavern wrecks and night dives.

Los Bajos in Bahia de Ocoa, is an isolated dive site with a large fish population, and **Barahona** further to the west, is an area being developed for ecotourism and the diving sites are rarely visited at present. Wrecks of both ships and aircraft can be seen.

The reefs of **Puerto Plata** and **Sosúa** have been damaged, but the waters are suitable for training dives and Open Water certification, while **Silver Bank** about 80 miles (129km) north of Puerto Plata, is one of the largest coral reefs in the Caribbean. It was here that a salvage company discovered the 17th century *Concepción*, a Spanish galleon laden with silver coins, many of which were found encrusted in coral.

Samaná and **Las Terrenas** offer the largest concentration of wrecks off the coast. It was off Samaná that the galleons *Conde de Tolosa* and *Guadalupe* were salvaged.

The country's first marine park has been established off Cabo Caucedo, south of the international airport.

La Caleta National Underwater Park offers both shallow and deep diving with reef and wreck dives, night dives and fresh water caving all possible. There are two wreck dives: the *Hickory*, an iron ship used for many years to explore the wrecks of Spanish galleons, is a 200 foot (61m) long vessel lying in 55 feet (17m) of water and now itself attracts the attention of divers; a few minutes away by boat is the second wreck lying in 100 feet (30m) of water.

The reefs off **Miches** and **Monte Cristi** also have a number of wrecks and are the target of salvage operations.

Dive companies and dive schools include:

Actividades Acuáticas,
Dominican Adventures,
Calle César Dargam 20,
Santo Domingo,
(☎ 540-4194)

Gus Dive Centre,
Roberto Pastoriza,
Plaza La Lira 11,
Santo Domingo,
(☎ 566-0818)

Mundo Submarino,
Santo Domingo,
(☎ 5660-0430)

Punta Cana Diving Centre,
Punta Cana Beach Resort

Tropical Dive Centre,
Las Terrenas, (☎ 589-9410)

Tropical Lodge,
Samaná, (☎ 538-2480)

Tennis

There are many courts on the island and several are floodlit. Book a court early in the morning or late in the afternoon when it is cooler, unless you are well acclimatised to the heat.

Water Sports and aquatic activities

All resorts and most large hotels offer a range from Hobie Cats, jet skis and windsurfers to kayaks and Sunfish. Experts are often on hand to teach you how to sail, water ski and parasail. Water skiers must always operate well away from swimmers.

The north and north east coasts offer excellent conditions for **windsurfing**, and the world championships were held at

Fact File

Cabarete in 1987. The resort has many hotels which specialise in windsurfing packages, although conditions are only suitable for experienced boarders.

The powerful Atlantic breakers also provide excellent conditions for surfers, especially around Rio San Juan and Cabrera.

Yachting, marinas and berthing facilities

There are marinas at Boca Chica and Boca de Yuma; La Romana, is the home of the Club Nautico de Santo Domingo, (☎ 566-4522)

Telephones

The international code for the Dominican Republic is 809. From the U.S., dial 1-809 and the seven digit number. From the U.K. and Europe, dial 001-809 + the seven digit number. To ring the U.S. from the Dominican Republic, dial 1 + area code + seven digit local number. AT&T's U.S.A. Direct (card calls and collect) is available throughout the country. Dial 1-800-872-2881 for the operator. For Sprint dial 1-800-751-7877

To ring the U.K., dial 011-44 +area code+seven digit local number.

Although the country has a modern telecommunications system, and there is international dialling, if staying in a hotel, most international calls have to be made through the hotel switchboard and a hefty premium is added. You can make calls from the offices of Codotel, the privately-owned national telephone company, found in all towns and cities. If you need to make a call, go to an empty booth in one of these offices, make your call and when you have finished, settle up with the desk. These offices are usually open daily from 8am to 10pm and later in large cities.

Time

The Dominican Republic operates under Eastern Standard Time Zone and daylight saving is in effect year-round. This means that from late spring to autumn, the Dominican Republic has the same time as New York and is five hours ahead of London (i.e. when it is noon in London it is 7am in Santo Domingo) and from late autumn to spring, the time in the Dominican Republic is one hour ahead of that in New York.

Tipping

Tips are generally added to restaurant bills as a service charge of 10 per cent on top of the 8 per cent government sales tax. Always check to see if the service charge has been added, and if not it is usual to leave a tip of 10 per cent or more if you feel like it. It is customary to tip bell hops in hotels, maids, taxi drivers, guides and other people providing a service. Tip taxi drivers around 10 per cent and bell hops $1-2 for each piece of luggage.

Tourist Offices

The main tourist information centre is on Avenida Mexico near its junction with Avenida 30 de Marzo, Santo Domingo (☎ 221-4660). There are also information centres at Puerto Plata on Long Beach (☎ 586-3676), and at the Town Hall in Santiago.

Overseas Tourist Offices

Toll free travel information can be obtained by ringing the following telephone numbers:

U.S. ☎ 1-800-752-1151
Canada ☎ 1-800-563-1611
Spain ☎ 900-995087
U.K. ☎ 0-800-899805
Holland ☎ 06-022-3107
Germany ☎ 0130-815561

U.S.
One Times Square, 11th Floor, New York, NY 10036.
☎ (212) 515-4966

Canada
2355 Salzedo Street, Suite 307, Coral Gables, Florida 33134
☎ (305) 444-4592

Canada
2080 Crescent Street, H3G 2B8 Montreal, Quebec, Canada
☎ (514) 499-1918

Tour Operators

U.S.

Alken Tours
☎ (718) 856-7711

Barceló Tours
☎ (305) 374-0045

Fling Vacations
☎ (215) 266-6110

Fact File

Friendly Holidays
☎ (516) 358-1320

Globetrotters
☎ (617) 621-9911

MK Travel and Tours
☎ (305) 441-7600

Roca Tours
☎ (305) 599-9400

T For Travel Tour
☎ (305) 642-9999

TBA Tour and Travel
☎ (305) 532-8899

Travel Impressions
☎ (516) 845-8000

Wyder Tours
☎ (305) 373-8687

Canada

Adventure Tours
☎ (416) 967-1510

Canadian Holidays
☎ (416) 620-8050

Fiesta Holidays
☎ (416) 498-5566

Regent Holidays
☎ (416) 673-0777

Vacances Air Transat
☎ (514) 987-1616

Weddings

The Dominican Republic is a popular destination for honeymoon couples, and other couples get carried away by the romance of the island and decide to marry while on vacation. If you decide to marry, you can enjoy a traditional church ceremony, or make your vows on the beach, on a luxury yacht or in a flower-bedecked gazebo by a sparkling hotel pool.

Many hotels and resorts specialise in weddings and honeymoon packages, and have staff experienced at helping with all the formalities and arrangements.

Weights and Measures

The metric system is generally used for weights and measures, although you might come across some old Spanish measures and U.S. ones. Motor fuel is sold in U.S. gallons, while cooking oil is sold by weight in pounds, as is most rum, beer and other liquids.

LANDMARK
Publishing Ltd ● ● ● ●
VISITORS GUIDES

* Practical guides for the independent traveller
* Written in the form of touring itineraries
* Full colour illustrations and maps
* Detailed Landmark FactFile of practical information
* Landmark Visitors Guides highlight all the interesting places you will want to see, so ensuring that you make the most of your visit

1. **Britain**

Cornwall	Hampshire
Cotswolds &	Jersey
Shakespeare Country	Lake District
Devon	Peak District
Dorset	Scotland
Edinburgh	Somerset
Guernsey	Yorkshire Dales & York

2. **Europe**

Bruges	Tuscany & Florence
Provence	Madeira
Italian Lakes	Lanzerote

3. **Other**

Dominican Republic	Florida Keys
India: Goa	Florida: Gulf Coast
India: Kerala & The South	Florida: Atlantic Coast
Gambia	Orlando & Central Florida
St Lucia	New Zealand

Landmark Publishing
Waterloo House, 12 Compton, Ashbourne,
Derbyshire DE6 IDA England
Tel: 01335 347349 Fax: 01335 347303
Catalogue sent on request

Index

A

Agriculture	44
Aguas Blancas	104
Alcazar Museum	71
Altos de Chavón	98
Amber	112
Amber Coast	105
American stewardship	37
Arawaks	28
Avenida El Conde	68
Azua	92

B

Bani	90
Barahona	93
Bavaro	101
Boca Chica	96
Breadfruit	48

C

Cabarete	114
Carnival	42
Casa de Campo	98
Casa del Cordon	69
Catalina Bay	100
Catalina Island	100
Catedral de Santa Maria de la Encarnación	73
Cayo Cabrito	109
Church of Santa Barbara	69
Climate	13
Coconut tales	50
Colegia Santa Clara	76
Columbus	26
Conch shells	58
Costambar	109
Costanza	103
Caribs	29

D

Drake, Sir Francis	74

F

Faro a Colon	78
Felix Maria del Monte	42
Food and drink	46
Fortaleza Ozama	76
French occupation	33
Fuerte de la Concepcion	69

G

Getting around	87
Government	46
Guácara Taina	79
Guaguas	89

H

Haitian invasion	36
Hato Mayor region	102
Higuey	101
Hospital Iglesia de San Nicolas de Bari	77
Hurricanes	14

I

Indians and Cannibals	28
Industry	45
Inglesia de los Remedios	72
Isla Cabritos	93

J

Jacagua	106
Jarabacoa	104
Jaragua National Park	94
Jardin Botanico Nacional	79
Jimenoa Waterfall	104
Juan Dolio	96

L

La Atarazana (Dockyard)	71
La Romana Region	97
La Vega	105
Lake Enriquillo	93
Los Haitises National Park	116
Luperon	109

M

Malecon	80
Manchineel	20

Manuel de Jesus Galvan	42	**O**	
Manzanilla	108	Ocoa Bay	92
Mercado Modela	80	Oviedo	94
Merengue Festival	42	**P**	
Minerals	45	Palacio Nacional	81
Mirador Park	80	Panteon Nacional	72
Montasa Isabel de Torres	113	Parque Independencia	68
Monte Cristi	108	Parque Nacional del Este	100
Museo de Arte Folklorico	106	Parque Nacional El Morro	108
Museo de las Casas Reales	72	Parque Zoologico	82
Museo Nacional de Historia y Geographica	81	Pedernales	94
Museum of Dominican Man	81	Pepper sauce	59
		Peravia	92
Museum of Marine Archaeology	71	Plantain	56
		Playa Dorada	113
Museum of Natural History	81	Playa Las Terrenas	117
Museum of Pre-Hispanic Art	81	Plaza de la Cultura	80
Museum of the Dominican Family	77	Puerto de San Diego	72
		Puerto del Conde	68
Museum of Trujillo	81	Puerto Plata	111
		Punta Iglesia	94
N		Punta Rucia	109
National Aquarium	81	**R**	
National Parks	25	Rainfall	14
Nutmeg	53	River Yuma region	100
		Rum	63

S			
Samaná	117		
Samaná Peninsula	116		
San Cristobal Province	90		
San Pedro de Macoris	97		
San Pedro del Macoris region	96		
Sanchez	116		
Santeria	41		
Santiago	106		
Santo Cerro	105		
Santo Domingo	66		
Sosúa	114		
Spanish conquest	32		
St. Francis Monastery	69		
T			
Taino	28		
Taxis	89		
The Alcazar de Colon	69		
The Pedernales region	93		
Theatres	82		
Tobacco	107		
Torre del Homenaje	76		
U			
Universities	44		
W			
Whales	117		

Published by: **Landmark Publishing Ltd,**
Waterloo House, 12 Compton, Ashbourne
Derbyshire DE6 1DA England

1st Edition

ISBN 1 901 522 08 3

© **Don Philpott 1998**

The right of Don Philpott as author of this work has been asserted by him in accordance with the Copyright, Design and Patents Act, 1993.

All rights reserved. No part of this publication may be reproduced, stored in a retrieval system or transmitted in any form or by any means, electronic, mechanical, photocopying, recording or otherwise without the prior permission of Landmark Publishing Ltd.

British Library Cataloguing in Publication Data: a catalogue record for this book is available from the British Library.

Editor: Nicki Knott
Print: Editoriale Libraria, Trieste, Italy
Cartography: James Allsopp
Designed by: James Allsopp

Picture Credits

Casa Marina Beach Club, Sosúa: 6/7
PHOTOBANK: Front cover, 23B, 115B
Gran Ventana: 18M
Don Jaun Beach Resort: 18M, 30T, 31B
Riviera Beach Hotel, Barahona: 22B
Puta Cana Beach Resort: 30B
Parado Naco Beach Resort: 30M
All other photographs supplied by the author

Cover Pictures

Front: Confresi, Beach Musicians
Back cover above: Casa Marina Beach Club, Sosúa
Back cover below: Sosúa, Fruit vendor on the beach

DISCLAIMER
Whilst every care has been taken to ensure that the information in this book is as accurate as possible at the time of publication, the publishers and author accept no responsibility for any loss, injury or inconvenience sustained by anyone using this book.